ONCE THERE WAS A VILLAGE

ST. MARTIN'S PRESS · NEW YORK

Yuri Kapralov

ONCE THERE WAS A VILLAGE

St. Martin's Press
175 Fifth Avenue
New York, N.Y. 10010

The years are so much different from one another. Some will come and go like a spring shower with a clear sky to remember them vaguely, others move slowly, every day an eternity and nothing gets done. Things happen one year, the grass grows taller. And some years it's just not worth getting out of bed.

Strange thing time. You don't have to catch it and eat it; time is relative, it's where you're at that counts when you're an artist, but it's still very strange. Especially when you're locked into a landscape where nothing appears moving, yet you know everything is moving and everybody is alive, even the dead. Underneath the thick layers of paint, between the brush strokes, among the red bricks and gray concrete, the black window gates and fire escapes, on the rooftops and the empty lots, in the garbage cans and in our narrow hallways. The time moves, a stray cat pouncing on anything it can catch with the quickness of an outcry. Always moving, healing some wounds, opening others.

Once There Was a Village

In the summer of 1966, we moved from a small four-room apartment on Seventh Street near Avenue D to a larger, sunny four-room railroad flat on Seventh Street between Avenues B and C.

For us, it was a great improvement. Our new building was exceptionally clean. No more puddles of urine and bags of garbage and dog shit in the corridors. No more going past abandoned iceboxes filled with mice, and burnt-out mattresses. It was cheaper, too—we paid forty-two dollars a month for the new place and almost fifty-seven for the old.

At that time, except for an old Spanish man on the top floor, our new tenement building was Slavic. There were three Polish families, a Russian couple, a Slovak family. The super was Ukrainian, and the lady who shared his apartment and did most of his work was Carpatho-Russian.

The super didn't want to rent me the apartment. He was hoping for some nice Slavic family and here was this bearded guy who said he was a Russian artist. Very suspicious. He kept looking at my beard, I guess he wanted to touch it to see if it was real. I spoke Russian to him, but he kept staring at me refusing to believe he'd heard the words I was saying. He finally mumbled something about how I didn't really want to rent the apartment because it had gas heaters—it cost too much to keep warm in winter. Which was true enough.

Dora, the Carpatho-Russian lady, liked me right away. She told Freddy, the super, to go downstairs and take a nap. The apartment was mine, she declared, anytime I wanted it. After she met my wife and my son, she was elated. She talked to us for a couple of hours and made us feel at home. Freddy too softened somewhat. I bought him a bottle of good vodka and from that moment on, grouch that he was, he never gave us any problems.

The apartment itself needed a lot of work. It was filled with cheap ancient furniture and all kinds of junk—old trunks from Russia, clothing, small pieces of fur from some pitiful animals including three dried-up foxes, bedsprings, chests of drawers, hundreds of other things.

Once There Was a Village

No one had lived in that apartment for over two years. The woman who did live there had gone back to Germany. For some reason she kept up the rent, mailing checks to our landlord until something happened to her a few months back.

Freddy and Dora took some of the furniture down and stored it in the street near our garbage cans. I took down the rest. Within an hour everything was gone from the street. We had to tear off the old linoleum (a backbreaking job), paint and plaster the place, buy a used icebox, get our landlord to install a stove. It took us at least two weeks to get the place in shape. It was worth it though; not many apartments in New York had so much sunlight.

Our next-door neighbors—there were two apartments on each floor—were a family of Polish immigrants. The man was good-looking and healthy-looking, around thirty. His wife, quite the opposite, looked plain, sickly, and a lot older. They were religious people—the priest from St. Stanislaus Church visited them on Sundays, sometimes accompanied by one or two nuns.

They had four daughters. Three were small—four, five, and six. The oldest was eleven. She went to St. Stans parochial school, spoke some English, and acted as an interpreter for the family.

When we moved in, they regarded us with curiosity, suspicion, and a trace of hostility. Within a month or so, I became friendly with the man. There's nothing like sharing a couple of cans of beer on the fire escape during our hot summer to bring people together. The woman remained cool and distant.

Sometimes I'd take my wife and son to the East River Park, and our neighbors would be there too, having their own picnic, enjoying their day off. The father would be sitting in the shade, drinking his beer and watching the boats, and the girls would be running around nearby, playing ball. The father was working as a gravedigger for a cemetery in Long Island City. He was making eighty-five bucks a week, according to Freddy, who had never made half as much in his entire life and was envious.

One evening, the father and I were drinking beer on our fire escape. He was moody and upset. He mentioned he liked my son and he wished he had a son too. I told him there was still plenty of time.

We first noticed something unusual when the girls next door began coming home very late at night and sleeping most of the day. And their mother would cry her heart out for hours. We could hear her through our livingroom walls. I didn't see the man for a while, but I was working then and coming home too tired to think of anything. Dora told me one morning he was in a hospital. I couldn't believe it. I couldn't imagine a guy like him being sick. But, as it turned out, the man had cancer, and in a few months he died.

The mother had a hell of a time getting on welfare. She almost went back to Poland.

I remember how bewildered I was when I found out that the man had died. He seemed so healthy, so happy. I knew he had cancer, but cancer can be cured. Even when I was walking around the neighborhood trying to find a florist, I kept telling myself it couldn't happen. I did find a florist at Fourth Street and B, bought a large bouquet of gladiolus. I didn't know how to approach the woman without making her feel worse. I knocked and hoped she wouldn't open her door. Our apartment doors open into our kitchens. Hers was sparkling clean that day. A beautiful embroidered tablecloth covered her small table, bread and fruits were arranged in a wooden bowl, and next to it was a small bunch of lilies of the valley. The crosses and the holy pictures on the walls looked bright in the afternoon sun, there was not one trace of gloom. As if she was expecting people for Easter Sunday.

There were two nuns sitting in her kitchen. Evidently her daughters had been sent away. I was embarrassed seeing the nuns unexpectedly and so close. They were both very young and had wide Slavic faces. They stopped reading whatever they were reading, from a black book, perhaps a New Testament, and watched me curiously. I handed the woman the gladiolus, said something stupid, and jumped back to my own apartment. After the nuns left, she stopped by and thanked us.

Her friends, the Polish family on the second floor, had recently bought a large house somewhere on Long Island and offered to rent her three rooms. Of all the people in our building, I liked that family the least. They were snooty to us and everybody else in the building. The man was one of the few Slavs who had it made. He was a foreman in some construction company. Yet, with all the money he was making, he still sent his wife to work—cleaning offices at night. They had a blond teenage daughter, nice-looking, but she had a hard, lean, almost whorish expression. And her boyfriends driving up in their souped-up '57 Chevys had that same hungry look that later became the look of the junkies. The father had a new Oldsmobile station wagon which he washed religiously every Saturday. They were tightfisted with their money. Dora told me once, laughing, that they would leave her and Freddy fifty cents each, in separate envelopes, every Christmas.

The reason they were offering to rent three rooms to our neighbor was not altogether friendship. They needed someone to help pay the mortgage. And the rent they wanted was no peanuts, two hundred dollars a month. Quite a jump from what the gravedigger paid when he was alive—$36. But the poor woman really had no choice. She couldn't stay in our neighborhood alone with her four daughters. And since she was now on welfare and, ironically, getting much more money than when her man was alive, she decided to accept the offer. Both families moved to Long Island.

I believe she made a mistake, moving in with the people from the second floor. All the other tenants thought so too. Only the woman's priest thought it would be a good idea.

The apartment next to us was empty for a few months. It was strange not to hear the little girls scream and play and

6   *Once There Was a Village*

run up and down our stairs. We were also beginning to feel apprehensive—everyone in the East Village knows it only takes one bad family to fuck up the whole building. And we had two empty apartments now, bad news.

We were relieved when two single men in their late forties, Mike and Bill, rented both apartments. Mike rented the one on the second floor and Bill rented the one next to us.

Once There Was a Village

That was in the early spring of '67. Things were relatively quiet on our block, save for occasional fights between members of two Puerto Rican clubs, family squabbles, and the burning of mattresses and abandoned cars. The Great Hippie Invasion had not yet begun. There were fewer than twenty junkies living on the block, and while burglaries were frequent, muggings were rare. The ethnic composition of our block was fairly evenly divided three ways: the Slavs, the Puerto Ricans, and the bohemians. The latter group included many black-and-white couples and families, some leftovers from the Beat Generation, some students, and a few hippies. It also included a good number of hardworking, struggling, creative people—artists, writers, actors, composers, musicians. Aside from these main groups, there were a few Jewish and Irish families and about a dozen winos living in an old Ford in a parking lot across from our house, and in various cellars.

The Slavic group was the largest and also the least visible. They were the poorest and the most oppressed. They had the misfortune of being devoutly religious, and their churches, with their archconservative bishops and priests and parochial schools, exploited them far more than the System itself, mainly by teaching them to accept with grace all the shit handed them and to be eternally thankful that they lived in America. Humility was of the essence. It didn't matter that you cleaned office buildings all your life, or washed dishes or dug graves. It didn't matter that there was not enough decent food on your table, nor enough money to buy decent clothing or an old TV set—that the only home you could afford was the forty-dollar-a-month apartment you were in now, or the sixty-dollar apartment you'd eventually move to in the Greenpoint section of Brooklyn. It didn't matter that your daughters would never go to college and your sons would later get blown up in Vietnam. What mattered was that you had to be very quiet and never raise your voice, because you were living in America the Beautiful. And, incidentally, you were white.

The Puerto Ricans on the block who were Catholic, along

with some Slavic and Irish families, belonged to St. Brigid's Church. It was a good church. Rather than giving out fire-and-brimstone sermons, its priests concentrated on helping the poor to survive. Father McDermott, an idealistic and warm man, later expelled from that church for his too-liberal views, worked hard at organizing the Brigade In Action, one of the few antipoverty outfits that really functioned. He also worked with the older people and teenagers. He still lives and works in the community.

The majority of the Slavs were older people living on Social Security. In larger and younger Slavic families, men were usually factory or restaurant workers and women worked as cleaning ladies in uptown or downtown office buildings, or as waitresses. Very few were on welfare, as far as I knew, although most of them were certainly eligible. Our super, for example, was getting around seventy bucks a month from Social Security and another six (yes, six!) from our landlord for his work. And being super at that time involved a lot of work. We had an ancient coal stove for the hot-water boiler, which alone required hours and hours of work each day just to keep the water warm. The basement was always flooded, and he had to push the water and mud with a broom toward the main drainpipe. There were other things to do, too.

There were Slavs on our block who looked down on Puerto Ricans and there were Puerto Ricans who looked down on Slavs. Yet, on the whole, the two groups got along remarkably well. There were several intermarriages and many lasting friendships, especially among families who had lived in the same buildings for many years. The bohemian group kept to themselves and somewhat above the other two. They were disliked and envied by both the Slavs and the Puerto Ricans. The bohemians were the most affluent, and prime targets for burglaries. I also suspect that about half of our bohemian population did not really HAVE to live on our block, and that was strongly resented by the people who really did have to.

Bill and Mike were of Slavic descent. Bill was a second-generation Russian, a gentle, plumpish man with a clubfoot. It was difficult for him to climb three flights to his apartment, so he was always resting on the stairs. Sometimes he'd knock on our door and, after apologizing for several minutes, shyly ask me to get him some groceries. Whenever he'd do that, he'd make me feel like I was doing him the greatest favor in the world. The first few times, he'd even try to give me a quarter or fifty cents for doing it. And he would never ask for anything unless he really was in trouble, or too tired to do it himself.

He helped out during the Sunday services at the Russian cathedral on Second Street. He had a night job somewhere, I think it might have been at the VA hospital, and every morning around six, rain or shine, I'd hear him, his clubfoot scraping the old linoleum of our stairs, returning home.

Bill had a sister and a brother who lived on Staten Island and whom he dearly loved. He'd bring us beautifully painted Russian Easter eggs prepared by his sister. Sometimes Bill would just stop by for tea and conversation. He was terribly lonely. He enjoyed his new apartment because most of his difficult life he had lived in a small room at Second Street and Avenue C, in very unpleasant circumstances. This apartment was no more expensive than his room, and there was so much sunshine and air. A world of difference! Bill was very pleased with it and was fixing it up, little by little.

Mike was Bill's neighbor in their old house. I believe Mike was Polish, but I never did find out. Mike was a very heavy drinker. He told me that he and Bill simply had to move out because somebody was setting fires in their building. And indeed, a few weeks after they had moved, their old building burned down.

About a week or two before Mike and Bill moved into our house, the Russian couple on the second floor moved to a smaller apartment at Sixth Street and First Avenue. They

Once There Was a Village

were a strange couple. The woman had a vicious German shepherd who once nearly killed my dachshund. The man she was living with was a former officer in the Soviet Army. During the Second World War he was captured by the Germans and almost died in POW camps. Toward the end of the war, he had joined the Russian Liberation Army of General Vlasov—the army of doomed men who put on German uniforms not because they liked Germans, but because they knew they'd die in POW camps sooner or later. This was a way out. And many joined for idealistic reasons—they hated Stalin much more than the Germans. The man on the second floor was captured by the Americans, narrowly escaped forced repatriation back to the U.S.S.R. and certain death in some concentration camp, and eventually, under an assumed name, managed to come to the United States. He was also a heavy drinker. Not as heavy as Mike, but then I never saw anybody who was. He'd often lose his temper and bellow at poor Freddy, who was afraid of him. "Janitor! Come here, swine," he'd yell, and the building would shake. And Freddy would run up obediently and listen to the man's insults and complaints. Dora was not so easily impressed. She'd yell back at him the Russian equivalent of "go fuck yourself, old horseradish," or she'd just ignore him.

He had terrific fights with his woman, and I guess he'd beat her up from time to time, judging by her screams. I think the man is dead now. I think they're both dead because at first I used to see her with the dog in Tompkins Square Park and him playing cards with other old men, and I haven't seen either one for some years now. And the only way older Slavs move out of the East Village is through Jarema's or Wolinin's funeral parlors. Or some less popular funeral parlors. Mostly it's Jarema's.

Into their apartment moved, surprisingly enough, an Irish family: a grandmother with fluffy white hair and a grandmotherly face; her son, a heavily overweight man about forty; and his two teenage sons. The younger boy was soon helping Bill with his groceries on a regular basis. Then Bill picked up the Hong Kong flu and never recovered. He even fell on the stairs once. He stayed in his apartment and refused to see the doctor. He said he couldn't afford one. And he died.

His brother let us pick out what we wanted from Bill's furniture, and we took a large, well-made wooden closet which we are still using.

By now, our block had changed considerably. The Great Hippie Invasion was in full swing. They came in by the thousands; they camped in almost every hallway. And with them came the reporters and the photographers and the camera crews and the motorcycle gangs and the revolutionaries and the plain idiots and just about every imaginable and unimaginable kind of freak. A battalion of cops set up a Command Post by St. Brigid's School at Avenue B. Antipoverty groups sprang up like wildfire, but most of them were ripoffs and did very little good.

This was a time of renaissance for the East Village. Bookstores and head shops and even art galleries opened all over the place. The most remarkable place was the cooperative nursery next door to my house, opened by Jim and Mary Richardson, old friends of mine. Books could be written about this nursery. I'll only say that it was the most spontaneously HAPPY place for kids I've seen so far.

Another good place which opened up was Contact, just next door to the nursery. Contact was an emergency shelter for runaways and street people. Larry Zicht, another good friend, ran Contact with the help of a hippie commune then living on Fifth Street near Avenue C. Over the years Larry helped well over a thousand kids and many people on our block regardless of age or who they were. And Larry helped me too, more than once.

Contact was established on a shoestring grant, but it was a very effective operation. A storefront that used to be a toy

12   *Once There Was a Village*

factory, it was open to everyone. There was coffee and tea, peanut butter and jam, perhaps doughnuts or cookies. There was a makeshift medical room in the back, and a shower. The kids could relax there, even sleep if they wanted to, and many did. There were games available, a kiln, and a sewing machine. Dr. Lockwood came in once a week with her nurse, and she'd usually have at least twenty kids waiting to see her with all sorts of ailments, mostly V.D. and hepatitis. A psychiatrist and a psychologist also came once a week. The bulk of help, though, was in the form of Larry's counseling and getting the kids on welfare, into decent apartments, hospitals, and out of dangerous situations, like talking them out of committing suicide or leaving bad drug scenes.

Late one night, shortly after Contact opened, I was going past it when I noticed a couple of shadows in the back room. I tried the door and it was open. I turned on the light. There were three hippies huddled in the back room, shivering. It was a very cold night. They had nowhere else to go, so they broke into Contact. They begged me to let them stay and swore they wouldn't steal anything. They were from Cleveland. I turned on the radiators and let them stay. I knew Larry wouldn't mind. He didn't. He said this was what Contact was all about.

Jack Early opened his bookstore next to the playground. To me, it was the best bookstore in New York City; he had just about every paperback I wanted. Jack was doing all right for a while, paying his rent. One night as I was coming home late, there was a commotion near his store. Jack was helping some guy get in a car, the guy was bleeding. Jack told me, "Yuri, I can't take it, I just can't take it." I think he was crying. What happened was a gang of junkies, flying high, had wandered into his store and started stabbing everybody without any provocation, it wasn't even a hold-up. By the time Jack had grabbed his club and chased them out, several people were stabbed and I think one of the guys who was stabbed died later in Bellevue. Jack abandoned his bookstore and headed for California.

And Avenue C began having its summer riots. I'll never forget the first one.

It began Friday evening, around eight. A hot and muggy evening, our mosquitoes were biting harder than usual. Not one branch of the tree in our backyard was moving. The sky, purple and polluted, wasn't moving either.

And, as if to defy all the oppression surrounding her, a very old woman in a top-floor apartment across my yard climbed out on her fire escape and began washing her windows.

Then it came—the shouting of many voices coming from somewhere around Houston Street and Avenue C, like a huge wave breaking on rocks, another wave of voices, closer to us, and another, closer still.

Everyone on Seventh Street was now hanging out of the windows or on fire escapes, looking at the intersection of Avenue C. Everyone knew the rumors were true; the riot was on.

First we heard windows breaking, the popping of bottles. About a dozen small kids, none older than eleven or twelve, ran across the intersection throwing bottles, rolling garbage cans, and breaking the windows of a few cars parked near the intersection. They were the vanguard.

Next came two large groups of teenagers, some of whom were singing, some shouting and throwing bottles, some dancing. Some stopped long enough to set three cars on fire and build a mountain of garbage between Sixth and Seventh Streets on C, which they also managed to set on fire. They also broke into the small butcher shop near Seventh Street and threw broiled chickens, salamis, and pieces of meat to the cheering onlookers.

Right after them, four solid-looking dudes threw a thick rope around one of the gates of Romashko's Liquor Store on Seventh and C. A pickup truck, to whose bumper the other end of the rope was tied, appeared as if by magic.

It could have been a beautiful ripoff. Unfortunately, just at this time, four unmarked cars filled with plainclothesmen raced by Seventh Street toward C. The dudes dropped their rope and ran, and the pickup disappeared too, like it was never there.

The cops stopped a few buildings before reaching C, jumped out, saw what was happening. There was a good-sized crowd now at every corner, the cars were burning brightly, along with the garbage, bottles, and tops of garbage cans flying all around. And while the detectives stood taking in the scene, the kids on a roof nearby were zeroing in on them with metal milk-crates stored on the roof for just this occasion.

The detectives didn't waste any time; they jumped back into their unmarked cars and backed off full speed all the way to B. A couple of milk crates hit their cars, but most missed.

The crowds, however, suddenly dispersed, the teenagers stopped yelling and singing, even the sirens stopped. It was very quiet for a few minutes. Only the fires crackled at the intersection. Bottles popped now and then.

And the men from outer space—the Tactical Patrol Force in their weird riot-gear—were marching silently, in single file, on both sides of Seventh Street toward Avenue C, hundreds of them.

It seemed so unreal, like it was another time, another place. The same kind of unreality and near-silence when, after a day of bombing and an evening of rioting, the Germans quietly moved into my city. Now I am standing on my fire escape three flights up and I think I hear the heavy sounds of their soft rubber boots.

Someone throws a bottle from a rooftop across the street. Two or three more bottles. Very efficiently, a team of five TPF's runs into the building and up the stairs. End of story.

A full, science-fiction moon hangs over Avenue C. A few steps from the intersection, Father McDermott is talking to a group of four or five junkies, asking them to stop setting fire to a bunch of garbage cans next to a wall—the building might catch fire, people might die, and the TPF is getting ready to shoot all of them down anyhow.

Two more waves of teenagers race by. The TPF is ready and more than willing. The leaders are caught, beaten, and thrown into the TPF's station wagons. The rest are allowed to flee.

I am sitting on my fire escape, drinking beer, and I see something I just can't believe. The bottles and garbage cans are now flying again, TPFs are running back and forth, and kids have even managed to set a police communication truck on fire. And in the midst of all this, a contingent of the Petrograd Workers Commune, red and Vietcong flags waving, slogans and so forth, about fifty people, mostly white hippie-revolutionary types, are marching in the middle of Seventh Street from B and where are they going? To Avenue C. Everybody's astounded, and the TPFs can't believe it either. The marchers are also astounded as they begin to look around. I guess they've been to some demonstration and haven't heard what's happening. By the time they reach my fire escape, most of them seem to have gotten the message and the column is melting very fast. About a dozen of them, the ones carrying flags and slogans, march right into the middle of the intersection and try holding some kind of a meeting.

Once at the intersection—by now knee-deep in broken glass, with bottles flying, TPFs and kids battling it out with sticks, guns, and garbage-can covers, cars burning, a man lying in a gutter beaten half to death, and many other unpleasant things happening—the marchers finally realize that they are in the midst of something very closely resembling a real revolution, no bullshit. The marchers break up and run in all directions.

One of the TPFs ventures into the intersection to retrieve something the marchers dropped when they fled. He gets hit on the side with a garbage can cover thrown like a frisbee. He drops to his knees, and several bottles hit him and the cement around him. Two other cops jump out from under some building and drag him to safety.

Fewer and fewer bottles are thrown, as more and more TPFs get into the act. Three busloads arrive and park in the lot across from our house. I guess they're the reserve. About ten TPFs are standing across from the liquor store alone.

The TPFs seem to adopt a new tactic now. They've secured several hallways on Avenue C and a few hallways on Seventh Street by kicking everybody out and not letting anyone in, even if people lived in those tenements. This done, they concentrate on catching teenagers, any teenager that looks suspicious whether the kid was doing anything or not—and once they catch a kid, instead of arresting him, they drag him into one of these "secured hallways" and beat the hell out of him and throw the kid out the back door into the yard. And the kid barely makes it home from there, holding onto his balls and his ribs. And the next morning he'll be in a hospital. Simple and efficient.

When the media arrive, it usually means that the event is over. And the media arrive in full force—at least five trucks with TV campers, lights, and other paraphernalia, also individual reporters, cameramen and so on. I want to take my dog down for a walk and to rap with some friends who are down walking their dogs or drinking wine and beer on their stoops and discussing the events.

But this first, biggest, and best three-day riot on Avenue C simply refuses to be put down.

The word filters out on what the TPF does with the kids. Many brothers and fathers, even some women, come out in the streets with sticks, hammers, chains, whatever they can get hold of, and it's a whole new ballgame. A huge new garbage barricade is built across Avenue C between Sixth and Seventh Streets, while the TPF is afraid to interfere and people cheer. The lights and cameras were onto that action—a movie about the end of the world. Or the beginning.

A beautiful Puerto Rican girl, a good friend, cries and screams next to me—she's worried about her boyfriend, who's among the people building the barricade. I try holding her to keep her from running out there. I tell her that her boyfriend can certainly take care of himself. Another friend, a black musician from next door, is hanging onto her other arm and we are also holding our dogs on leashes and our dogs are getting scared and some asshole is throwing bottles right into our crowd, and the TPF is going into action—they line up like a wall with their sticks, guns and masks, facing us; they're ready to charge us.

Some guys jump up on a couple of TV trucks, push the newsmakers aside, overturn the cameras, kick out the lights, and at the same time, the TPF charges us—men, women, children, dogs—and our bunch is herded into some basement full of some ancient boxes. We're still hanging onto the girl and she's still crying about her boyfriend; our dogs are howling. Next to us is a Puerto Rican woman with two frightened kids about eight, another black guy and two black women, an old Ukrainian woman mumbling her prayers and crossing herself, four wide-eyed hippies, and three TPFs who yell at us and shove us and tell us to move, except there's no place to move to.

One TPF places his large revolver in the middle of my musician friend's forehead and tells him he'll blow his head off if his dog bites him. My friend's dog is a saluki (an African dog, not big at all), she's a gentle animal—her teeth are chattering from sheer terror. My dog, a dachshund, is also shaking like a leaf and I am beginning to itch and my friend with the gun stuck to his head is uneasy, and the kids and women are screaming. Only our Puerto Rican girl stops crying and looks around, like she sees the scene for the first time. And here's where I made my mistake.

Somewhere in my brain sat a jerk who kept telling me, "Look, this can't be happening. This is America, the land of the free, not Russia or Germany. They just can't shoot somebody because they want to. There must be a reason for all this. Reason, that's the password. I'll reason with this motherfucker."

And I said to the TPF holding the piece, "Look, officer, sir, there's no need to get excited . . ."

Well, he did lower the gun. The other cop, however, whacked me hard with his stick on my thigh (he meant to hit me on my balls, luckily I half-turned and he missed); then, like in a slow-motion movie, he took a big swing and zapped me on my stomach with that same heavy stick. I saw stars, millions of them. I knew I was going to throw up and, so as not to throw up on people, I turned and leaned on some boxes; my head was almost next to the wall.

While I was throwing up, I noticed that there was a black hole in the wall right next to my head. Like there was a wall safe there before, and someone took it out. And in the blackness, in that hole, lay something. I couldn't tell what it was, but there was SOMETHING.

The TPFs were soon called out and they stupidly told us to remain in the cellar, or else. Else what? Anyway, we busted open the back door and got out into the house. I felt like I was about to pass out so I took my dog home. The Puerto Rican girl agreed to go to her mother's and my musician friend, hopping mad, went to get his own piece.

At least half of Avenue C was now burning—an awesome sight. New groups of kids and adults were battling it out with the TPF without the slightest intention of giving up.

The intersection of Sixth Street and C was one giant lake with an empty fire-engine partly submerged in the middle of it. The garbage barricade between Sixth and Seventh Streets was still holding and burning in spots. Another weird-looking army was moving up from Houston Street—Sanitation Department trucks, cranes, forklifts, and sweepers—all of it protected by a wall of cops.

The news media have split. I have no idea what time it is, must be pretty late and my thigh aches, but my mind is now wide awake. I am beginning to feel new energy, there are places I have to go, people I want to see. I leave my dog at home. I am back on Avenue C.

In two minutes the situation has changed again. I stop just in time, behind the newsstand. From here I see that TPFs are grabbing everybody now. There is a sightseeing bus parked near the Eighth Street intersection and when the TPFs grab somebody, they stuff him into that bus.

I go back through the building next to mine, through the backyards, climb our fence and two fire escapes, jump over a shaft full of garbage, rip my hand on some barbed wire, and finally make it to the back window of my friend's apartment. I knock at it and he opens it holding an ax. He's been ripped off six times, every time through that same window. He's surprised: "What the fuck are you doing here, why couldn't you go around like normal people?"

"Are you kidding?"

We smoke some grass, watch the sanitation department army cleaning up the débris. My friend's windows are right above Avenue C. TPFs are still running around in full force, catching stragglers and pushing them into that same sightseeing bus. These poor people will see some sights tonight for sure.

My friend is a young Ukrainian poet, Dimitri, who came to America when he was six. Here, he's lived only in the East Village, first on Thirteenth Street, then on Seventh Street, and now on Avenue C. He began working when he was twelve, finished evening high school, and went for one semester to City College. For the past few years, he worked as a clerk with the welfare department. Now, he's collecting unemployment and thinks he was fired because he's Ukrainian (white) and not a black or a Puerto Rican. He may well be right, but it's also possible he was fired for his drinking. He's stoned right now.

"Just look at those motherfuckers." He waves derisively toward his window and Avenue C, meaning the Puerto Rican kids.

"There'll never be a real revolution in America, you know why?"

I have a feeling he's going to tell me and I've already heard it ten thousand times.

I say, "Dimka, let's go to the roof, get some fresh air."

His apartment smells like shit.

He continues, "Because the Establishment's too smart and they're too dumb. The Establishment divides and conquers. The Establishment says to Puerto Ricans and blacks, 'You're the new privileged minority. You've suffered too long. All doors are open to you now. You form your own exclusive club—call it Third World people, call it what you like. No whites allowed. You talk about revolution, killing whitey, go to college, do anything you want. Here's the dough.'

"And then the Establishment says to the working class of America—to the Ukrainians and Poles, Italians and Russians, Irish and Germans, Carpathians and French and Portuguese, even to our Albanians—people who really built America with their sweat and blood and got fucked doing it; people who are still building it and keeping it together and still getting fucked by it, the Establishment says to them, 'Look at these Third World people. They got everything, you got nothing. You worked hard and you got nothing.'

"Listen, I heard about this program to help minorities at Columbia. I always thought I was a fuckin' minority. I figured maybe I could get in, surprise my mother, get a college education. So I had this interview with this spade faggot who was the director and a Jew dyke who was his assistant. The program didn't stretch to Ukrainians. Only to Puerto Ricans, blacks, Orientals, American Indians, and Eskimos.

"No, man, the Establishment's too smart to let people get together. It wants to keep us mad at each other."

"Who's your Establishment?" I asked.

Dimitri shook his thick black hair. He's a tall, muscular guy, a very dark complexion, Zapata mustache. He could easily be taken for a Puerto Rican, Mexican, or Indian.

He grins at me, almost whispers, "Fuck you, Yuri, you

Once There Was a Village   21 know, you KNOW."

We finally get out on the roof and Dimitri stares moodily at the garbage.

"You and Sara broke up?" I ask.

"Bitch went to California." He leans against the roof door and rubs his eyes. "That bitch . . . Yuri, you don't know, man, you've got a good Russian woman . . . you can't feel it, I gave that piece of shit my soul . . . I haven't got my soul any more, there's nothing here, nothing, you understand?"

He slaps himself on the chest a few times to underscore his emotions.

"You can't understand. I was true to that bitch. I wasn't fucking anybody else. She was fucking everybody, but I was true, I was true."

"That's your tough luck. What are you going to do now? Sit in your filthy apartment and count cockroaches?"

"I don't know. I want to relax and sleep, you know, just like Lermontov said, somewhere under an oak tree."

"You're full of shit." We're speaking in Russian, by the way.

"I don't tell you how to live, you don't tell me how to live. You're an artist, you know nothing about reality. To you everything's a painting . . . one of your stupid piano constructions . . ."

"Listen, Dimka, I don't put down your poems."

"This is useless," Dimitri said, and took a leak into the darkness below.

On the roof next to ours, separated by a narrow ledge, there was great activity, something like a church bazaar. Kids were running back and forth with cartons of shoes, shirts, and liquor they had ripped off, which they were selling to adults. I asked a Puerto Rican man I knew from Seventh Street how much he paid for the two bottles of Scotch he was holding. "DOS PESOS!" That did it for me. I left Dimka and balanced my way over the roof just in time to buy the last bottle.

That roof was actually a double roof. It was high in front,

even with other roofs on the block, but in the back, it was one floor lower. On that lower roof were at least twenty people, some drinking beer and booze, some smoking grass, some dancing. They were really enjoying themselves. Most were teenagers, but there were some adults among them. The majority were Puerto Ricans; a few were white and a few black. They evidently knew one another well, it was like a special private party. I didn't want to stare. I made my way back to Dimka, who was still thinking about something. We drank our Scotch, sat around for a few more minutes, and then climbed down to his place. I was going home when I remembered that hole in the wall of that cellar.

"You got a flashlight?" I asked Dimitri.

He had one. Instead of going home, I decided to check out that cellar.

I didn't go to the cellar right away. Dimitri went to sleep, and I sat on his fire escape until it got gray. All kinds of thoughts were coming and going through my mind. My thigh and my stomach were aching again. I was drinking Scotch and not getting drunk. I had the strangest premonition that once I got into the cellar, a thread would break and my life would somehow change.

And it was supposed to be bad luck to return to such a place anyway. I thought of going home, getting some sleep—the Scotch was finally beginning to work. My stomach felt nice and warm. Had I stayed on that fire escape another fifteen minutes, I wouldn't have gone to the cellar. It was getting noticeably light now. I was relaxed. I felt like washing the night out of my mind, like doing a few pen-and-inks and, later on, taking my son to the East River Park and taking a nap on the grass.

Dimitri wasn't far off wanting to sleep forever under some oak tree. Sleep, however, as Lermontov said, "not with the sleep of death but with all of life's forces running through you, all your senses attuned to the wonders of nature." I felt that way myself. Only I wanted to make sure I could get up any time I wished.

I was finally getting high, about time. I climbed down and went to find that cellar. I thought it was on Avenue C, but after I got out in the street, I realized, of course, the cellar was on Seventh Street.

It was almost morning now. TPFs were standing like statues. I had the feeling they were not going to bother me now. The sightseeing bus was gone. I went past them, turned the corner on Seventh, went into the hallway and into my tiny cellar.

Today, whenever I pass that cellar, I don't even look at its new metal door. It's now rented for storage by a Puerto Rican street-mechanic called Pinto. And the opening in the wall, that hole I was staring at, has been made into a safe again—a homemade kind of safe. Pinto cemented the walls, attached a steel door, and hooked a big lock into it, the kind you don't break off, period. And to get to that safe, you'd have to move tires, tools, and car engines. Pinto keeps his gold there—holy medallions he buys, rings, bracelets, watches, and his .32, with small supplies of heroin and coke which he sometimes deals.

When I got there during our first riot, the smell of burned garbage was very strong. A couple of rats ran around chasing something and scaring me half to death, and a dog howled in the hallway upstairs.

There was a couple of inches of soot in my hole in the wall. Underneath the soot was that something I had seen, or thought I had seen, when I was throwing up. I pulled it out. It was a small old leather briefcase, the kind they don't make in America. There was nothing else in that hole. I put the briefcase under my shirt and got the hell out of there.

I don't know what I expected to find in that briefcase. I had heard stories of people finding EVERYTHING in their basements and between their walls—skeletons, booze from the Prohibition era, jewelry, guns, money. I was hoping it would be full of money—nice old twenty-dollar bills, even ten-dollar bills, even fives, even ones. As soon as I was home, I double-checked the doors and windows and

Once There Was a Village

poured the contents of the briefcase on top of a large piano construction I was working on at the time.

There was some money in my briefcase—six dollars in single bills plus some change that fell out of one of the pockets. The rest were documents, visas and birth certificates, lots of writing, some photos and two drawings, pencil drawings—very childlike. One drawing depicted mountains and the other a ruin of a house by the side of a road with some trees.

The papers were in Hungarian, German, and English, while all the writing was in Russian. It was a kind of sporadic diary and last will and testament of a Carpatho-Russian immigrant named Stephen Lechko, who came to America in 1908 when he was thirteen years old, exactly a year after the rest of the people in his village, including all of Stephen's family, were massacred by Austro-Hungarian soldiers on a punitive expedition into the Carpathian mountains.

Stephen went back to visit his native country in 1960, came back, and died in his tiny apartment on Seventh Street in '63. He died of unknown causes, and his partially decomposed body was found when neighbors complained of the stink and the howling of his dog Taiga, an orange mutt.

While Stephen was back in Carpatho-Russia, in the summer of 1960, he wrote, aside from the account of his journeys, a half-poem, half-story which he called "Once upon God's Green Earth Stood a Beautiful Village."

As every Russian boy knows, Carpatho-Russia is a very strange land where witches and vampires fly freely and even worse things come out of their graves on Black Sabbath, and, not incidentally, the wicked sorcerer from Gogol's "Terrible Vengeance" met that wonderful knight somewhere there, and the knight opened his eyes and lifted the sorcerer up to heaven and then threw him into the very depths of hell, also somewhere there.

A tiny country, for centuries ruled by foreigners of different and hostile religions. Always oppressed—its villages and towns plundered, people massacred or taken into slavery, churches leveled, Orthodox priests put to work as horses to pull Catholic priests' carriages, its harvests stolen, its leaders skinned alive.

There's still a large Carpatho-Russian community here in the East Village. Several churches, the largest of which is at Tenth Street and Avenue A. Quite a few social clubs, self-help organizations, and funeral parlors. It's a community of mostly older people living their last years in hopeless poverty and degradation. There are no antipoverty agencies helping them and never will be. The younger Carpatho-Russians live mostly in New Jersey, Pennsylvania, and Ohio. They are not doing too badly. A lot of them work as carpenters; some work in factories and some in the mines. I've met quite a few Carpatho-Russians on Seventh Street. The lady who did most of our super's work, Dora, was from there, and she often talked to me of her homeland, which she tenderly referred to as *moy krai rodnoy*, "my dearest region."

The villages and the valleys and, of course, the mountains were so beautiful, Dora told me, there was nothing like them in the entire world. The air was clear. People were kind and gentle. Should a stranger enter one's house, he'd be fed and taken care of better than the host himself. It was unthinkable to steal or not to help another family in need. The sunflowers grew eight feet high around houses and the tomato plants even higher.

I never lived in a village for any length of time, so I can't fully understand the peasant's love for the land, yet there's something so strong and spiritual about it that it transcends the continents and the years and dies only when the peasant is buried. And maybe not even then. When I read Stephen Lechko's "Once upon God's Green Earth Stood a Beautiful Village," I wanted to translate it right away, word for word—the first time and the last time I ever wanted to translate anything. I didn't do it.

About a year later, his briefcase, along with some of my paintings and constructions, were lost in a fire. This, then, is his story, not word for word, but as I remember it.

Once There Was a Village

Once upon God's Green Earth Stood
a Beautiful Village

The sun is high, the sun is low.
God only knows where the sun wants to go.
Over the mountains, over the river, over our valleys,
Over our bridge.
Over our village, two hundred people.
Over our church with a light blue steeple.
Over our house the sun once stood.
Over our cows and our fruits.
Over my sister and my mother, over my father
And my three brothers.

It was the time of the Holy Trinity Festival. Our village square was decorated with ikons and flowers.

It was a good summer.

It was a good year.

We had meat, flour, honey, butter, and beer.

Twelve babies were born and we had four marriages.

My father bought a seven-string guitar at Lvov's market.

Our neighbor, the blacksmith, repaired our plows and our cart.

We have finished digging a new well behind our garden.

We have finished the hiding place for storing our food. This time the collectors and their dogs would not find it! This time it was in a very good place, a ravine near our small forest.

They would not be able to find our food even with their dogs because we grow poppies of the mountains all around and on top of it. When the dogs get into a field of mountain poppy, they get wild and can't smell a thing.

We had no partisans living in our village, although we fed them and gave them warm clothing when they were passing through our village to hide in the mountains and forests.

Two policemen on horseback came to check on us every few days from the railroad station seventeen kilometers away.

We had a new doctor who visited our village every week and whom we suspected of being a government spy. But we had nothing to hide. Except our food.

A long gypsy caravan passed through the village one day. That was not so unusual because there were many gypsy tribes living in our region.

It *was* unusual for the gypsies not to camp out by the river for an evening or two of dancing, fortune-telling, and other entertainment. It was MOST unusual this time because the year had been exceptionally good and everybody had some money. And there is no person in the world who parts as easily with his money as the Carpatho-Russian peasant after only two glasses of vodka.

Yes, it was most unusual for the gypsies to ride over our bridge and not to stop until they were out of sight.

The older people were worried—they believed that when the gypsies hurried, bad luck was not far behind.

The following day, while my father and my brothers were working in the cherry orchard on the other side of the village, I ran off with the rest of the boys to play near the forest.

We were going to play soldiers—there were twelve of us, we divided into two armies. Since I couldn't run very fast—one of my legs was shorter than the other—the leaders threw bones to see which army would have me. One group went across the village. My group stayed near the forest.

We lay in the grass and talked about how we were going to sneak up on the other group and what we would do with the prisoners once we'd caught them. We had sticks and slingshots, our leader had a folding knife, and we had collected some good stones.

It was still early in the morning. It was a warm, pleasant day. We were talking of all the likely places our rivals might be hiding when we heard shots. Many, many shots and bursts of machine gun fire. We knew it was from machine guns. We were not dumb. The shots were all coming from the village. We were about half a kilometer away from it, separated by a field of rye and some apple orchards. All my friends ran to the village immediately. Since my house was almost on the outskirts of the village and not too far from where we were, I decided to climb a tall pine on the edge of the forest to first see what was going on.

I climbed very high until I could see the entire village and even the houses on the river. I had never seen so many soldiers before. There were perhaps two thousand of them. They were running from house to house, shooting people down and setting fires. Twenty soldiers advanced through the field to meet my friends, who were running toward the village. They shot all my friends dead and kept advancing to the edge of the forest until they were right under the tree on which I sat. They stopped and turned back. Another group of soldiers in gray uniforms (the first group was dressed in dark blue) came with stretchers. They took the bodies of my friends and carried them to the road where now stood a long line of canvas-covered, horse-drawn wagons.

More gray soldiers were coming with stretchers full of bodies, and they were emptying these stretchers into the wagons. All of the village was now burning and when I turned toward my house, it, too, was burning.

Near the river were a few houses toward which the soldiers did not advance as yet. Two groups of partisans armed with hunting rifles and sabers, each group thirty or forty men, crossed the river in several rowboats.

While some partisans were fighting off the advancing soldiers, the others were helping fleeing people to get into the rowboats. I knew right away what their plan was—to hide the people *v kamyshah*, in our marshes where grass is so tall you could stand up and no one would see you.

Another group of partisans, about fifteen men, came out of the forest. They ran past me and attacked the gray soldiers who were still picking up bodies in the orchards. I wanted to climb down and join them, but I was afraid.

The soldiers saw the partisans and ran away to their wagons, but other soldiers in dark blue appeared with two machine guns on small wheels, and the battle raged until all the partisans were dead.

Along the river, the battle was not over. Partisans were in four houses closest to our pier and they were shooting at soldiers, killing some of them and stopping their advance.

A new column of soldiers arrived across the river. They stood in a single line as far as the eye could see and held their rifles ready to fire. They also rolled out two machine guns. Another group of soldiers in dark blue was advancing on the pier from my direction; they were also rolling a machine gun.

They began shooting from across the river at the people in the boats and near the boats. Our river is only seventy or eighty meters wide, so right away they killed most of the people. Those they did not kill, the blue soldiers killed with their bayonets. The partisans in the houses were still shooting and the soldiers were throwing grenades and torches into these houses.

There was much black smoke and loud explosions. And even I couldn't see very clearly what was happening. All that time, the gray soldiers were collecting and carrying the dead and dropping them into the wagons.

After some of the thick smoke cleared, I began crying because I knew that no one in my village was alive.

Except me.

It all happened so very, very fast. It was not noon yet. Had we played our game, it would not yet be over.

I wondered why no one in the village had seen the advancing soldiers.

How did they sneak up on us in such a way?

The gray soldiers went through the village and the orchards and the fields three more times, picking up more bodies, making sure not one body would be left behind. The soldiers in blue rested in small groups on the ground.

Some new wagons arrived and they, too, were soon filled with bodies.

30   *Once There Was a Village*

Every house in the village was burning and the smoke was rising all the way to heaven.

The church was burning, too, but still standing. It was the only building in our village with brick walls. Two officers started throwing grenades into it until the walls collapsed.

I didn't see the body of the priest, his wife, and his daughters. It was hard for me to recognize the bodies, I was too far away. But I knew they were dead long before the church was gone.

I liked very much the priest's daughter Marfa, who was only two years older than I was. It was because of Marfa that I decided to become an altar boy (there were four of us), and I was trying to be a good student in our school. Our teacher, too, was dead. He was from Great Russia and he always argued with the priest. He was a good man; he beat up his students only when he was drunk. And his wife was dead, and his baby. I think I even saw his body being thrown into one wagon. Him or somebody else with a red beard.

And dead was the blacksmith who told me funny jokes and promised my father he would teach me his skills. My father thought it would be a good occupation for me because of my limping.

I didn't want to think of my family although I knew they, too, were all dead.

I didn't want to think of my family for a long time afterward.

After they put all the bodies in the wagons, the soldiers in gray rounded up all the livestock they could find except chickens and geese. Then they went once more through the village and found two more bodies. They loaded these bodies. The wagons made a wide circle in the wheat field not far from my house and they rode toward the railroad station followed by a column of gray foot soldiers, a larger column of dark blue soldiers, three wagons in which wounded and dead soldiers were riding with the machine guns, and about ten soldiers in gray, riding our horses and herding our livestock.

One unit of blue soldiers, about thirty men, remained in

the center of the village, by our fountain. They put up three tents; their cooks built a fire and began preparing a meal. Three soldiers were walking on guard, the rest were lying down near the fountain or cleaning their rifles.

I didn't know what time it was. The sky was beginning to darken. Most of the houses were still burning, but not as brightly as before. My body was numb from sitting on the branch for so long. Both my legs were asleep. I couldn't cry or think any more. I was hungry. It was safe to go to our house now. I climbed down, fell, and scraped myself. I was cautious. I began crawling through the field of rye toward my house.

It was even darker now. I could see the first stars. It was quiet except for the loud conversation and singing of soldiers. They were Hungarians.

Everything surrounding my house had stayed as it was. My house was built from very good pine logs with oak crossbeams and a straw roof. The roof was long gone, and most of the pine logs turned to charcoal. Only the oak beams and some things inside were still burning and smoldering.

I heard very quiet barking and whining and was surprised to see my oldest brother Vassily's dog, a black puppy called Sharik, tied by his rope to a cherry tree in our garden. I untied him. The dog licked me and jumped with joy. I had to put my hand on his mouth to keep him quiet.

I noticed that our small shed, in which we kept tools and food for our two cows, was still standing. It was very low —the lilac bushes around it saved it—no one could see it from the house. There was enough straw there. It made a comfortable bed for myself and Sharik. I was not hungry any more, only very tired. We went to sleep together, close to one another.

Very early in the morning, we were awakened by more shooting. Again I climbed high in a tree, an apple tree near the shed, and again I had a very good view of what went on.

Partisans had attacked the remaining soldiers and taken

Once There Was a Village

them by surprise. They killed most of the soldiers and captured a few. I am an old man now, but to this day, I can still hear the agonized screams of those captured soldiers as they were tortured before being put to death.

I did not go to the partisans. I don't know why. I took Sharik and walked first to the place where we were hiding our food. I took several pieces of dried beef, some pork fat and flour, and some honey. I packed it into a small burlap bag. I ate some beef there and fed Sharik too.

Then we both walked past the tree on which I was sitting yesterday, around the forest, two kilometers down to the river bank where I used to fish with my father and my brothers and where our boat was tied up. The boat was there and the oars were still in it.

> *The Sun is high, the sun is low,*
> *God only knows where the sun wants to go.*
> *God sits higher than the sun,*
> *But God is asleep most of the time.*
> *Gone is my village with all its people.*
> *Gone is our church with the beautiful steeple.*
> *Our blood runs deep into our earth*
> *And over our blood soon the sunflower grows.*
> *Its petals open wide as an innocent soul.*
> *Swallows fly around it and bees.*
> *The nightingale will sing to it in the evening.*
> *AND THE SUNFLOWER OF OUR SOULS WILL*
> *BE HAPPY.*

No sunflowers around here.

Just garbage-filled backyards and hallways. Empty eye-sockets of abandoned tenements and synagogues. Burnt-out cars. Asphalt, brick, and cement. Broken glass and charred plywood and not enough air to breathe.

Frightened people. Angry people. People who can't be bothered.

And the souls wounded by heroin and despair are still dying.

Streets are almost empty.

It's nine or ten in the morning.

That peculiar smell of burnt garbage clings to the fire escapes.

It's already hot, maybe ninety degrees, maybe more.

I catch the beads of sweat running down my nose and rub them all over my beard and my face. I am sitting on a bench behind our bandshell in Tompkins Square Park.

I am numb. I wish I were sleepy. I wish I could stop thinking. Far too many threads are connecting the past and present and running into the distance to catch the very uncertain future.

A neverending canvas.

An abstract, painted as if by chance. Only the colors are real—bright yellow and blue, dark red and burnt sienna. Love, hate, peace and violence, life and death, freedom and oppression. The gods locked in a struggle. I can't see who is winning. I am confused. I can only see the colors. The colors are the only thing I believe in. The colors are my reality.

What about this morning?

An old Ukrainian lady is feeding pigeons in the park, as always. On Avenue C, they have boarded up every store, swept up all the garbage, towed away all the burnt-out cars.

Old Slavic men are gathering in their corner of the park, not far from where I am sitting. I can hear some of the conversation at one of their tables, in Russian and Ukrainian:

"Well, the lads ran free last night . . ."

"Such robbers!" This was said with admiration.

"They should send them all to Russia. In three days they will behave as though they were made of silk . . ."

"Shut up, old half-idiot, and shuffle the deck. Let us play 'sixty-six,' I am tired of playing 'fool' [Russian card games]."

"You are a fool . . ."

"They should shoot a few."

"You forgot how we, too, once were fighting."

"Yes, but in those days, they did not hesitate to shoot us. I have a bullet scar on my thigh to prove it."

"Please, don't make him prove it . . ."

Two black guys walk by. More fragments:

"So dig, this dude puts on his rubber glove and tells me to bend down. I tell him, man, I am just looking for a job . . ."

Too late!

A red-haired plump lady with her three poodles is coming down my path from Avenue A, and a homosexual from my block called Sailor is walking his Yorkshire terrier from B. They have both seen me and are converging upon me.

Sailor is Spanish from Spain. How he wound up living here and why is a mystery to me. He's a very nice man, studying in some acting school and collecting welfare. He comes up to me first:

"You know, Yuri, I was ripped off last night, no kidding. Right in the middle of the riot. I was standing with a friend on my stoop and when I got back, everything was stolen. My radio, my alarm clock, my jewelry, even my kitchen utensils. Oh, and my suit, and I had nine dollars in my jacket. And you should see the mess. And here's a bit of poetic justice —they took my old TV set. I was going to throw it out anyway, it hasn't worked in years, but it was so heavy! Would you believe? It was my own fault, my own fault! I left the back window open."

"I believe," I tell him, "I really do. At least they left your dog."

"Jose was with us downstairs. Where's your Sieglinde?" Sieglinde is my dachshund.

"Home."

"Such a lovely dog."

Stella arrives, the red-haired lady.

"Hi, hi, how you been?"

"Some night," says Stella. "And, believe me, it's far from over. The worst is yet to come!"

"I think it was quite poignant." Sailor doesn't like Stella and her poodles. "Kids fighting pigs armed to the teeth and building that barricade. Almost like a painting by Delacroix, quite a heroic thing to do."

Sailor is somewhat into art, and whenever he's around me, he's dropping the names of famous artists. I think he's got some of them mixed up—once he spoke to me at great length about Cézanne's waterlilies.

Stella is getting mad: "You call looting and burning heroic? These punks were on a rampage. You know what they did to the bakery and the butcher shop? It's disgusting, we're becoming a nation overrun by savages."

"What do you mean, overrun by savages?" I say quietly. "Just take a look at all these cops."

On the corner of Avenue B and Seventh Street, the TPFs are holding their morning formation, at least a hundred of them. And four police are parked in front of St. Brigid's Church. Plus another bunch of cops, about twenty of them, are walking toward B through the park.

"Stella, you don't know what you are talking about," Sailor says. "These kids were not simply looting stores and setting fires. It was a political act, not some savages getting together for good times."

"*You* don't know what you're talking about. How long have you lived here?" asks Stella with some relish.

"Ten years."

"Then you don't know what you're talking about. I was born here and grew up here. This used to be a nice place to live. We were poor, yes, but we never had to lock our apartments. We had no thieves."

"But you had no heroin," I say.

"That's right. We only had liquor."

"I think Sailor's right, it sure took guts to build that

barricade. I was really proud to see them do it."

"But, Yuri, you didn't rush out there and help them do it," says Stella.

"No, it happened so suddenly and we didn't have time to do anything. I mean, we all stood and watched, like it was some movie, and then they chased us into a cellar. Maybe next time I will join them."

"And get yourself killed? So, you think you'll join them next time? They're all Puerto Ricans and blacks; you're Russian, you're white."

Stella has been mugged. More than once. Whenever she sees Puerto Rican kids walking down the street, her first thought is about her purse and the knife held to her throat.

"I am a true Caucasian," I answer slowly and distinctly.

That's my private little joke—I grew up in the Caucasus, I am a Kuban Cossack. This, I believe, makes me one of the few real Caucasians around. When I first came to America and couldn't speak any English, in all the forms I had to fill out stood that dear-to-me word "Caucasian." I thought that America was full of my countrymen until some jerk explained to me that "Caucasian" simply meant white.

Well, baby, I am not that white. Ever since I got to America back in 1949 and started washing dishes in Bolan's Restaurant in Nyack, most of my best friends have happened to be black. And there are Puerto Ricans here whom I can trust with my own life. I wish I could say the same for any whites I know (American whites).

Stella is right, though, in what she's carefully not saying. Too much racial hostility is flying around. And we shouldn't have it. Not anywhere, but especially not here. Because we have the same heavy cloud of poverty hanging over us—Puerto Ricans and Slavs, blacks and Jews, good people and bad, young and old.

Later this morning, I am playing chess at one of the tables in the park with a friend of mine, Tom, a black guy who had begun shooting up a few months before. Tom has a beautiful mind. He's an excellent chess player. A year later, he will be dead.

Tom says, "I'm surprised it didn't happen last summer. What gets me, no one was killed. [Tom happened to be wrong. One man was killed, and a few people died later in hospitals.] When you have a situation, your back's against the wall, you've been promised this and that and nothing's delivered. Same shit year after year. Man, it had to explode. I wouldn't call it a revolution and I wouldn't call it a riot. I'd call it an uprising. Now, if cops killed somebody, then you'd have a revolution. If cops start shooting, there'd be a real war. There will be an explosion like you would not believe. The whole country will blow."

The *Daily News* printed a short article about "The Disturbances on Ave. C." "Disturbance" was the word used in other papers and TV. DISTURBANCE!

Rumor has it there will be some shooting tonight for sure. That's why police snipers are on the roofs now and police helicopters are hovering back and forth.

The day moves on slowly.

I do get out with my son to the East River Park for a couple of hours.

What a relief!

We play ball, wrestle on the grass, watch the baseball game, watch the passing boats.

On the other side of the East River, among factories, shipyards, and tenements, a large green dome with Russian Orthodox crosses, a cathedral in Greenpoint, another Slavic section—Poles, Russians, Ukrainians, Carpatho-Russians. A step up from the East Village. I read somewhere there's supposed to be almost a million Slavs living in New York City alone and fifteen million scattered all over the United States, and three or four million in Canada. Truly, they are as a good Russian proverb puts it: "quieter than the water, lower than the grass."

I am worried about my unemployment checks running out next week. That's so stupid! Who knows what'll happen next week? Who knows what will happen tonight?

Once There Was a Village

But my worry is nagging. No jobs anywhere. And all this running through the uptown galleries showing slides of my work. What a waste of time! And they all say, "Your work is good, but . . ."

I realize, of course, it's not so much a question of talent but whom you know. So, big deal! What else is new?

I have to get some money somehow. And I have to get it soon. Going to the docks at night is no answer. The pay is good, three dollars an hour, but I went there five times and was only hired once, for ten hours.

I look at a large white cabin cruiser sailing by. Happy people sitting on deck, drinking something good. They wave at me and my son and we wave back.

I am thinking that these people probably have some pretentious shit hanging on their walls, while here am I, great talent and so on, and I don't even have enough bread to buy me a can of beer. Maybe I'll raid my son's jar of pennies again.

Then I remember the six dollars and some change which came out of that briefcase and is still lying on top of my construction.

Great!!!

Steve Lechko, you may be dead and buried, but tonight, you'll make me a very happy man. I can get a whole quart of hundred-proof vodka at Astor Liquors for four bucks.

The evening falls, and everything is quiet on C.

Cops are in position in the hallways and on the roofs.

Buses from the Department of Correction wait silently on Avenue B, near Ninth Street.

People sit on their stoops here and there, talking in low voices.

The darkness falls and the riot, or uprising, or revolution or whatever, begins again. Not as strong as the previous night, but strong: Molotov cocktails are being thrown along with everything else. The fighting rages at the intersection of Seventh Street and C and all the way up and down on C. Police cars and stores are burning, sirens are howling

—shouting. Police reinforcements are rushed in from their staging area at St. Brigid's School.

It gets quiet again around two or three in the morning. The vodka is beginning to hit me. I am finally falling asleep.

I am almost asleep.

It's very quiet now and it's beginning to rain.

And I hear the first shots.

Of course, the East Village didn't die right then. A few people were shot, the riot was eventually over, the liquor stores reopened, heroin, coke, hash, sunshine, mescaline, and grass were now sold openly all over.

A huge drug supermarket opened right on the block. I'd be sitting on my stoop with a couple of friends, eight, nine in the evening, and a well-dressed guy would walk by and he'd be singing, "Acid, acid, get your beautiful acid . . . only ten tabs left, beautiful acid . . ." Two minutes later, another dude, singing in a low baritone, "horse, horse . . . ride a pony, two bills, sweet smack . . ." Another five minutes, a small freckled chick about twelve would be dancing around, playing with her dog: "Jamaican, Jamaican, anyone for grass? Ten an ounce, thirty cents a joint, California joint . . . three joints coming right up . . . thank you very much . . . grass, grass . . ."

And you could simply buy whatever your heart desired, heroin to mescaline, from seven- or eight-year-old kids riding on their bikes around Tompkins Square Park. You didn't have to buy it in the street at all—you could dial one out of maybe fifty numbers, order what you wanted, and they'd deliver right to your door. The one bad thing with home delivery was that you were running the risk of being marked for a ripoff.

Life went, more or less, back to usual. And I had to find somebody for Bill's old apartment next door.

I stopped at the nursery. Jim and Mary weren't around, but there were a couple of mothers working there and one of them needed a place. She had a five-year-old daughter, the same age as my son. She was getting separated from her husband, who lived across the street. She rented the apartment and was very pleased with it. She gave a few good parties, her daughter got along well with my son. She didn't live in our house long; I think it was less than six months. She fell in love with some guy and they all drove to California. Her former husband, who still lived across the street, advertised the apartment in the *Village Voice* and got three hundred bucks for it—actually just for her keys, which he had borrowed from me. It was the first time anybody had paid any bread for an apartment in our building.

The chick who bought it was definitely with it. She chipped the plaster off the walls, put a thick wall-to-wall carpet in the living room, and expensive linoleum in the kitchen, and had the place painted in decorator's colors. She had a new Maverick, she was into group therapy, speed, acid, hash, and whatever was happening. I thought, then, she really knew how to live.

Around this time, our super died.

I looked at him lying so quietly at Jarema's for a long, long time. Only when I noticed people looking at me did I realize I was crying. Strangely enough, I was thinking mostly of myself. Of the time when I'd finally freaked out and nearly committed suicide. And of the time I was locked up at the Bernstein Institute. Of the pretty nurses sitting by my bed when I was under constant observation. And of the Thorazine which began to blur my vision to the point that I couldn't do my pen-and-inks. And of the relatively happy times there when my wife and son would come for a visit and I'd teach him to play pool. And of the time I played bridge with three other suicidal patients until four in the morning. And of the time I walked back home on a very hot morning. It was so hot not a tree moved in Tompkins Square Park; not even a dog was in sight. I was walking in another world. I met Freddy the super that morning. He was putting out the garbage cans. He gave me a sly, knowing look and didn't say anything. I walked up the stairs and my dog began barking. My son was up and my wife cooked some breakfast. She was friendly and very nice, but there was a hard expression in her green Russian eyes. As though to her I was dead. Or should have been.

Freddy had worked all his life, and to the day he died, he never had a vacation. As a kid, he had worked on the farms in upstate New York. He had tried working in the mines, but couldn't take it for more than a couple of years. The last part of his life he had worked for a small building contractor and would have made carpenter's helper—if the owner hadn't retired. Freddy was not a great talker but he did talk to me once. I believe it was in the winter of '68. I remember the dirty snow on the ground and the mountains of garbage. We were looking at two abandoned cars being set on fire directly across from our house and Freddy told me his theory. He said that when they had tested hydrogen bombs, the earth had got knocked off its axis and was now drifting aimlessly in space. Very soon it would pass close to the sun and burn to a crisp. Just like the abandoned cars. And the reason no one knew about it was because all the governments of the world were in a conspiracy to keep this fact a secret so that the people would not behave wildly during their last few days. Freddy knew about it, however. One night, a messenger from another planet came to his apartment and told him so. He also gave Freddy a certain capsule to take when that time came and it would transfer Freddy to that other planet. Too bad Freddy never owned a TV set; he would have enjoyed watching *Star Trek*. He looked very clean at Jarema's, cleaner than I've ever seen him. He also looked peaceful. He probably had taken his capsule.

During the time I was in the hospital, the Polish family on the third floor had bought a house with another family in some Slavic factory town in New Jersey and moved out, the last Poles to leave. I loved that family. There were five of them. The father worked in a Brooklyn factory; the mother in a cafeteria downtown. They had two daughters, both gorgeous-looking, and a son who was in the army in Vietnam. They were beautiful, real people, all of them. The younger daughter occasionally babysat for my son. We all missed them. About six months later, we learned through a friend that their son had lost a leg and an arm in that goddamn war. And into their apartment moved a frail, overworked, and overworried Russian lady with a thirteen-year-old son.

Our block was changing and yet remaining exactly the same. Slavic and Puerto Rican families were leaving, and the Albanians began moving in. The Albanians were really poor, even compared to the old Slavs. Most of the hippies had left. A few freaks remained. Most teenagers on the block, both Slavs and Puerto Rican, who had somehow been making it before, started shooting dope. Heroin was so cheap! In the beginning of '69, one could buy a bag of strong shit on the corner of Seventh Street and Avenue C for a buck and a half. Of course, the price was soon raised and the quality went down.

AND THEN A WHOLE ARMY OF JUNKIES IN-VADED US.

The junkies brought a reign of terror of such proportion that if I'd collected all accounts of just the holdups and stabbings, it would have filled a good-sized book. I knew only one old woman on our block who had *not* been mugged. That was the Carpatho-Russian lady who was now our super. She always carried a big club. Fewer than 20 pecent of all apartments were NOT ripped off. I'd also make a conservative estimate that approximately one hundred people on our block felt the knife or looked at the gun, or both, in '69 and '70. At least twenty people were stabbed. At least five were shot. Three were killed, as far as I know. I don't know how many died in the hospitals later. Needless to say, the cops did nothing. At the height of The Season (the spring of '69), when four to six people were being mugged on our block EVERY SINGLE DAY, no cops were stationed anywhere past Avenue B. And, in response to residents' pleas to at least put one cop on the corner of Seventh Street and Avenue C, the idiot who commanded the Ninth Precinct at the time would reply that he had no manpower available. His manpower was sleeping in their patrol cars in the East River Park. Many people on the block began calling cops "pigs." And it sure is an accurate discription. Pigs and leeches. I mean, sanitationmen collect garbage every day and sometimes even sweep our streets. Firemen put out fires and occasionally save people's lives, even at the risk of losing their own. Most of our cops do nothing to earn their paychecks. And, ironically, they collect the biggest checks, not to mention the payoffs. Some do worse than nothing. After people have been ripped off, these cops lecture them about living in "such a bad neighborhood."

Not everything was glum though, even in regard to muggings. There were a few bright moments. A man who lived a few doors from me was just beginning to make love to his wife when he heard a commotion in the hallway and a muffled cry for help. He jumped up, grabbed his samurai sword off the wall and, completely naked, took off after the mugger. It must have been a magnificent sight. Here's this big guy chasing the mugger on Avenue C late at night. Naked, with a huge hard-on, his long beard waving in the wind, he swishes around a long samurai sword with both hands yelling, "Stop, mugger! Mugger, stop!" Of course, the mugger glanced back over his shoulder, dropped whatever he was carrying, and ran even faster. My friend chased him past a parked patrol car with two cops sitting in it, then lost him and walked back, still swishing his sword. He walked past the squad car with the cops—the cops didn't move while all this was happening—picked up the pocketbook the mugger had dropped, and went back into his house. And from that incident on, muggings in his house became rare.

Other houses weren't so lucky. In the spring of '69 we simply had no choice but to defend ourselves. We organized a block vigilante patrol. We pooled what weapons we had: a spear, a saber, a couple of machetes, a few knives, and lots of clubs. And we did catch a few muggers. And, after a couple of muggers accidentally fell off a roof, the word spread and the junkies avoided our block for a couple of months. In fact, for maybe a month, ours was the safest

Once There Was a Village

block in the East Village.

On top of everything else, we had a pyromaniac running around. He set fire to the great nursery next door and it burned out completely. What a rotten shame! He set fire to Contact. Fortunately, only the two back rooms of Contact's storefront were damaged; five of my paintings in there were burned also. As far as I know, he burned one store on Avenue B and four stores on Avenue C before someone caught him. He turned out to be a kid in his early teens.

During this time the Slovak family on the top floor finally moved out. They had lived in our building almost eighteen years. They were a good, simple family. The man was a factory worker. He was STRONG. He had white hair and a red face and was of small stature, but you'd look at him and you'd just know he could beat the shit out of you or anybody else. Sometimes he'd invite me upstairs for a drink and instead of pouring a shot, he would pour a full glass of Imperial or Four Roses. The lady worked at night. They had two sons. One was married and lived in Brooklyn; the other, the younger one, was afflicted with some blood disease and always stayed in the apartment. He was in his late teens, a talented, sensitive boy who I hoped would continue painting and drawing and go on to become a good artist.

One night the lady was returning home from work and her husband couldn't meet her, for some reason, on the corner of Avenue B, as he always did. Two small kids jumped her by the playground, knocked her down, and took off with her purse. She was never very healthy to begin with, and after that incident she was sick most of the time and afraid of her own shadow.

They moved to a new apartment house somewhere in Queens. They came back to visit friends from time to time. They did not like their new neighborhood and it was very expensive to live there. But they felt they had to move. Here it had become far too dangerous.

A very good friend of mine who is both an artist and a belly dancer took their apartment.

In the late spring of 1969, when the New York *Times* was

reporting in depth on the evils of the East Village, describing "teeming tenements of Ninth Street between Avenue A and B" (yes, between A and B), I even thought of writing a letter to the editor to remind him that's where Tompkins Square Park is, stupid, THE WORLD FAMOUS TOMPKINS SQUARE PARK! The *Village Voice* came out with a cute description of our area, east of Avenue B: "Apeland."

APELAND?

It's so inaccurate! We have at least seven dogs for every ape. Anyway, at the time, I was a dog.

"Yuri, baby, what's happening?" my speed-freak friends used to say, and shiver, and grab their own dogs by the collars so that the dogs wouldn't jump up and run off somewhere.

My other friends used to simply cross the street and walk very fast in the opposite direction whenever they saw me. And the Ukrainian grandmothers sitting and chatting in the sun on the stoop across from my house would stop talking and look at me sadly and sigh.

There had to be something odd about my appearance, but I can't say for sure. I hadn't looked in a mirror for a while.

I'd increased my daily intake of beer from three to five quarts. That still didn't help soothe my nerves. And through some strange chemical process to which I am willing to swear, my output was exactly twice the amount of intake.

That's probably why I had my water-related nightmares. Like, I was in the old Fort Knox stockade and they were trying to drown me in the toilet bowl, and all the water moccasins converging on me while I am helplessly sinking in a Fort Jackson swamp, and water rats eating away my insides. Things like that.

I believe I was going coconuts.

I was walking again through the old Avenue B theater (thank God it's now the American Nursing Home!)—Loew's Avenue B—I still have the beautiful marble plate with a Cupid and a flower from one of your ladies' rooms. THE GREAT AVENUE B, an enormous empty palace with a gaping hole instead of a stage and thousands of rats living in its basement.

You could only get there through one of the doors facing Fifth Street and only at night.

My friend Emilio decides not to break open the door and, when I do break it open, he decides to wait for me outside. I go in, idiot that I am. Stairs, rats, pieces of broken glass, bricks, marble plates, boards, and a couple of junkies snoring in the back behind a mountain of broken seats.

Avenue B must have really been great when Jimmy Cagney was coming to settle the score with Humphrey Bogart. Kids must have been screaming their heads off and running back and forth to buy popcorn and candy, and it probably had a wonderful stage show, too—with clowns and magicians and singers.

I stop just in time, the stairway ends right under my feet. Nothing but blackness leading to the other side of the earth. Outside, Emilio is getting nervous. I am somewhat nervous myself. And cold. I should've taken my flashlight. I hear steps. Many steps. Too late. Help! The darkened theater is coming back to life. And it's not the ordinary abandoned moviehouse I thought it was but an ultramodern place straight out of some Stanley Kubrick movie. It has many stages and orchestra pits and screens arranged around a blue swimming pool. And a pleasant loud voice begins talking about some foolish drama they're about to present.

A strong current of warm air lifts me up on one of the stages, the lights go on, weird, unsteady lights. Sets, people, and decorations move around me, and I find myself right in the middle of some scene. And then another scene. "Enough," I yell, but it all goes on and on. Sometimes these stages are so crowded I can't even do my number. Other times, the lights leave my face and wander around, making no sense at all. The producers must have been tripping. And I am getting angry. At last! Everything is moving faster. Now I can take it!

A barrack-type house at the edge of a cornfield. Strange gurgling, sighing noises in back of the house, by the kitchen door. A wounded dog lies on the steps. A young, wild dog, red-haired, medium-sized, mean-looking, and strong. All night long I am digging shotgun pellets out of my dog's head and back. The dog recovers and runs off. A few days later, he appears again. This time, half his head is blown off and he doesn't recover. I deposit the dog in a roadside ditch near the Green River. Near another cornfield. Freeze frame, please, some funeral music.

A long-abandoned railroad track.

A few gray cabins. The track jumps over an ancient bridge and the line forks. One ends by the ruins of some warehouse, the other goes around a brown hill.

The metal sign turns and flickers red and turns again. That red is gray, too, and it's getting grayer.

Inside the motel, one room, a large double bed and a large chair. Two people are undressing, holding each other. He closes her legs so that her toes are touching. From her toes to her lips he kisses every inch of her body. All his muscles and nerves and every part of his soul are in her. He's frightened and hungry. Hungry for all the love he's missed. Frightened of so much involvement. Yet the involvement is now total. There's no way to shut it off. And the hunger is soon over.

The metal signs keep right on turning. In Cave City, in any city. And all the night managers look like Baptist ministers.

The end comes to everything, even to suburban shopping centers and used car lots, drive-in movies and bowling alleys, the funeral parlors which are themselves a real living end, and junkyards. The end.

A gust of summer wind burns my face. A cornfield rolls along the highway, and a forest pushes the neons aside. Louisville 24 mi. New Albany 19 mi. says the old sign. A few cars, an occasional truck. I climb under a barbed-wire fence and fall into the cornfield. Orange halo still hangs in the distance but right under my feet, some tiny animal runs fast and buries itself in the soft ground.

The cornfield, miles and miles of rolling, whispering waves. Another forest, this one is a mass of silence. "Come right in," it says, "I've been standing here always. And where have you been? You and your birches? I am warm and moist. I'll hide you well."

Maybe so, but the stars and the air feel much friendlier. And the stalks of corn move just enough to make out a beautiful primitive beat—one, two, a pause, three, four, five, and back to two. I sit down, close my eyes. It's a good thing I am so tired. I am passing out. Drowsy music, please. Green stars are dancing with yellow comets. I think, whatever the hell for, about driving my first car, a '40 Dodge two-seater with a large trunk, to a Russian Scout camp in the mountains of New Jersey. And a gray house owned by an elderly woman from New York whose son was a famous pianist. There's a piano in that house, on the first floor, surrounded by old armchairs and bookcases. The son arrives and plays. He plays for two hours, eats his supper, and plays two more hours. He is trying to impress a young Russian girl I fell in love with that summer. The gray house has a fantastic view of the mountains and the valleys and the Delaware River. Where is the pianist now? What was his name?

Silence.

A fresh, blue San Francisco morning. A small sailboat is going under the Bay Bridge on the way to Sausalito. It's nice and warm. I am dreaming, sprawled on the deck. My friend Hugh is at the rudder. Hugh's wife Mieko is cooking something delicious on her hibachi in the cabin. Hugh made the sailboat himself from an old surplus rowboat he bought for fifty dollars from a ship graveyard near Redwood City. Slow motion, please.

Once more, Mieko comes out on deck bringing some hot coffee. Closeup, please, hold Mieko's face—she's so beautiful. I think I'll give her one of my pen-and-inks.

Late at night, a large storefront on East Seventh Street between Avenue B and C is brightly lit up. In one of the windows a sign, "Contact," on top of the rising sun. Inside Contact, Alan and I are trying not to fall off the ancient stepladders.

We are stapling large strips of brown wrapping paper to cover the old walls in preparation for my one-man show. And drinking plenty of beer. A group of speed-freaks stops by, tries to break open the door. I explain, "Contact isn't open, will open tomorrow as usual at three in the afternoon. Right now, it's three in the morning." In the tenement building next door, in my apartment, my wife and Alan's wife are getting very mad. Possibly because they have nothing to drink and have run out of things to say to one another.

On Sixth Street, directly behind Contact another pair—a young minister and his wife—are quietly packing their books, records, and other belongings. They are from a therapy group I've attended a few times. They are leaving the East Village for good and going to another world, somewhere in Connecticut. They are in a pensive, nostalgic mood. Further down Sixth Street, in a luxurious—fantastic by our standards—apartment, another couple from that same unhappy therapy group is engaged in playing out an elaborate sex ritual.

He is kind of an artist and she's a combination artist, actress, writer, psychologist, and hooker. He's moaning and groaning and has no way of knowing that she has her mind set on moving soon to a much warmer climate—like Florida. And on Avenue C between Sixth and Seventh Streets, a good friend of mine is beginning to realize somewhere in the back of his mostly burnt-out brain that he's finally OD'd. He gets off his loft bed, crawls toward the window, and tries to break it open with his fancy cowboy boots. He almost makes it.

Back in Contact, we've stopped stapling brown paper on the walls. We sit on the table and drink what's left of the beer. Alan is talking about his trip to Europe, the life in

Once There Was a Village

Freiburg, various psychic experiments he's conducted, predictions he's made which turned out to be all too true, about the dream lab in Brooklyn and a book he's currently writing on psychic phenomena.

I talk mostly about my piano constructions. I have nothing else to talk about. We are having problems with our wives, but that subject is being carefully avoided. It's getting harder and harder for us to communicate, anyway; we are bombed. Outside, except for five or six stray dogs howling by the parking lot, Seventh Street is deserted. My wife finally comes down and bangs on the door. The lights go out in Contact. Ten more minutes and everyone is asleep. The pack of stray dogs moves on toward Tompkins Square Park, their yelping fading in the distance. Half an hour later, Dora, the super, begins mopping the stairs of my building, as she did every Saturday around five in the morning for many, many years.

Daybreak.

The morning of my show. Contact now resembles a giant paper bag filled with various constructions and sculptures. The constructions are hung on the walls, suspended from the ceiling, tied to the floor, on the tables, on the windows. They are made from old cash registers, shavings from picture frames, broken glass and beer-bottle tops, piano parts, leather from old suitcases, old jackets, glass from old-fashioned TV sets and beads, disks from thrown-out record-pressing machines, disassembled typewriters, dismantled pay phones, glass and wood from old telephone poles, many other things. Over all, there are at least seventy constructions, large and small. Plus, in the two back rooms, pen-and-inks, watercolors, drawings, oils, seascapes and nudes, and, finally, Russian fairy-tale-style oils painted on wood. Not a bad show, even if the walls had been white. In a paper bag it is much better because it gives the whole thing unity and a feeling of intimacy.

The show opens Sunday at noon and within two hours it evolves into a spontaneous, noisy, and gay block party.

Puerto Rican kids and teenagers run back and forth, bring their friends, ask me all sorts of tehcnical questions. Some people bring more wine and beer. Puerto Rican fathers and mothers sit around with the hippies and exchange their views. Ukrainian grandmothers come in bunches. Speed-freaks and ripoffs wander in now and then to check out the situation. One of my friends, who is a film-maker and lives next door, is shooting a movie of the event. Another friend composes a poem. Still another will write a short story about it. And people are buying the constructions and pen-and-inks. And this is fantastic! People from the neighborhood, very few of whom have any money to spend for nonessentials. Of course, the prices are low. Any artwork in Contact, for example, can be bought for less than one would pay for a rotten print in some plastic uptown gallery. And although most of the people who buy my constructions pay me in three or four installments, everyone pays.

The party lasts well into the night.

It is a very happy show.

Turn off the light, let's get out of here.

The First Dialogue between Psychiatrist No. 1, who has rather large purple wings and is hovering above my head, and me, sitting on top of a mountain made from my broken piano constructions.

NO. 1: I want you to realize I belong to the post-Freudian school of thought. I go more or less by intuition. Also, you'll find me different from other psychiatrists in this respect: I believe in talking, as well as listening. You can interrupt me any time you wish; after all, you're the patient. I believe we could relate to one another. I wasn't always a psychiatrist. In my youth, I studied singing and dancing. My wife is an actress. We have many creative friends. You've seen Stanley Kubrick's movies, of course, haven't you? We know Stanley quite well. I believe he now lives in England.

ME: I really wouldn't feel so bad if I only had a little money.

NO. 1: I believe we cannot afford the time to go back to your early childhood, so instead we'll concentrate, zero in, on your current hangups.

ME: Mind if I get myself a drink?

NO. 1: Yes, I do mind. And why do you drink so much?

ME: I am a Piscean . . . I guess I want to forget.

NO. 1: Forget what?

ME: I don't know, forget that I'm still around.

NO. 1: Where would you rather be?

ME: Oh, I can think of quite a few places.

NO. 1: Do you love your wife? [and speaking faster, chanting really] Do you take drugs? Do you love your son? What about your father? Where do you stand politically? Why do you carry such a big knife? Why don't you move to a decent neighborhood? Why don't you go to work for some advertising agency? Nothing wrong with making money, is there? Why are you taking apart old pianos and making your constructions? Why do your pen-and-inks depict only landscapes and seascapes? Why don't you do portraits? What do you think about Yevtushenko? Did you have a homosexual experience when you were a boy? Why did your father beat you up with his belt? Why do you hit your wife? Why did you try to strangle your first wife and beat up her lover? Do you get along with children? Which do you prefer, screwing or cunnilingus? Anal intercourse? Ever kill anybody? Do you wish to go back to Russia? Did you ever steal? Why did they put you in a stockade? Why are most of your friends black? Did you ever have an affair with a black woman? Oriental? American Indian? Indian Indian? Samoan? How old are you anyway? Why is your wife so hostile to me? Did you have a homosexual experience while in the Army? Do you like pornographic books or pictures? What sort of foods do you like best?

ME: [I wake up] Eggplant caviar! Sometimes called poor man's caviar. You take a couple of eggplants, two or three green peppers, couple of onions, a few cloves of garlic, one or two tomatoes, lots of spices, chop everything up and fry it in butter until the mush looks light brown like . . .

NO. 1:   [Interrupting, sadness on his face] Do you smoke grass? Hash? Do you masturbate? Frequently? You have any medical problems? How often do you take a bath? Would you like to see me once a week or twice a week?

ME: I really don't know . . .

A pink cloud is drifting toward them and envelops them. For a few seconds you can see the ends of the psychiatrist's purple wings sticking out; then they too disappear.

A Very Brief Call to Psychiatrist No. 2. It's exactly five twenty-five in the morning. One ringy-dingy, eleven twelve ringy-dingies.

NO. 2:   (Very sleepy voice) "Yes, hello?"
Heavy breathing and coughing on the other end.
NO. 2:   "What is it?"
Sound of a single shot, or possibly a firecracker.
NO. 2:   "Is anyone there?"
Silence.
NO. 2:   "Fuck you!" Hangs up, goes back to sleep.

April 8, 1969

A PETITION
To the honorable John V. Lindsay, Mayor, from residents of the block of East Seventh Street between Avenue B and Avenue C who have all been victims of burglaries and armed robberies.

Dear Mayor Lindsay:

We, the undersigned, are the residents of East Seventh Street. We have all been victims of burglaries and robberies. And many of us have been victims more than once. Some of us have been injured in these attacks. The robberies with guns, bayonets, and knives have increased frighteningly in recent months and all the bandits have been teenagers or young people on dope. Most of the bandits come here from the projects, but a few live right here on our block and we know who they are. There's no police on our block. The bandits watch for people coming from stores and rob them in hallways. They rob everybody. Puerto Rican, white, and black. Most of all, they rob old people who can't fight back. Soon, somebody is going to get killed. We need two cops on our block from afternoon until twelve at night. Their presence will help, for a start. Otherwise, we have no choice but to begin defending ourselves.

Mr. Mayor, help us soon!

B.D.: (Black, musician, composer, teacher. Address.) My apartment was burglarized of valuable instruments. I have been accosted on my way home from teaching and recording activities (I was able to rout them) and recently there have been, in the past two weeks, numerous suspicious fires in a nursery and in two apartment buildings. It would be good if action by proper authorities be taken before people begin to feel that they have been abandoned and will then have to find ways of protecting themselves and their property.

P.F.: (Address.) My black roommate and I were robbed in the hallway of our building by a black and a Puerto Rican youth armed with an eight-inch hunting knife. The incident was reported to the police.

R.W.C.: (Address.) I have been living here slightly over a year and in this time, my car was stolen, my apartment burglarized, and on three occasions, I have chased muggers out of the building *after* they held people up. In all three occasions the assailants were armed. Last week my apartment was partially destroyed by fires started under very suspicious conditions. There is and has been no meaningful protection by the police for myself and other residents of the block. Unless something is done to rectify this condition, we shall be forced to take

Once There Was a Village

matters into our own hands.

I.J.: (Hungarian puppet maker and performer. Address.) I was broken into, but only a radio and a TV were taken. I have been mugged once and injured and have also avoided numerous other muggings. If there is a window open for air, even when we are home, men always attempt to enter. I have finally boarded all windows up and even these are tampered with.

C.M.: (Puerto Rican, janitor.) This incident happened to me two weeks ago. When I came home from work, I was robbed by two men. One pulled a knife on me, the other just held me. They took twenty dollars from me. Everyone in this building has been robbed. (Address.)

D.W.: (Student. Address.) During the seven months I've been living here, my apartment has been successfully burglarized twice and to my knowledge, once unsuccessfully. A friend of mine was robbed in our hallway at gunpoint.

C.M.: (Black artist, bartender. Address.) Since my sublease tenancy, my apartment has been robbed twice and many, many irreplaceable items have been stolen.

M.Z.: (Ukrainian, dockworker. Address.) There have, in the past months, been three attempts to hold me up while I entered my building. It has in recent months become increasingly dangerous to walk on Seventh Street between B and C after dark. With the coming of the warm weather, tensions seem to be rising.

About twenty other similar accounts follow. The petition is sent to His Honor, the Mayor, in English and Spanish. A few weeks later two men do get killed as a direct result of these attacks. So far, and this is several years later, there has been no reply from the Mayor's office.

That spring, there were also two suicides and two attempted suicides. Three addicts died from an OD, and seven older people died from "natural causes" on East Seventh Street. Between B and C.

The two suicides were as diverse as anything can be. They even resulted in different kinds of death.

A woman who lived on a ground-floor apartment near Avenue C with her six or seven kids was found dead one morning. OD'd, I was told when they closed the doors of the ambulance. Strange. She was a very tough Irish lady with colorful tattoos on her arms and the face of a prizefighter who'd been fighting a good many years. Every time I stopped by to talk with her, she'd be pregnant. She sometimes helped Katie with her newspaper stand on Avenue C, before Katie sold it. I gave her some toys my son had outgrown and, in the hot weather, I'd often share a beer with her. She drank one hell of a lot. About a week before she died, there was a street fight and all her windows were smashed. I don't know much about that fight, looked about usual to me—people screaming and chasing one another with knives and bats and throwing tops of the garbage cans around. Anyway, it all happened so fast and it ended just as fast.

She was very much alive one day and the next day, they were wheeling her out. The old Jewish man from next door, who was a good friend of hers and used to babysit for her children, told me that her kids went to live with relatives

Once There Was a Village

upstate. And it wasn't heroin that killed her; she probably killed herself by taking half a bottle of barbiturates on top of a whole bottle of Seagram's Seven. There was a good reason for what she did, the old man said. He did not want to elaborate.

The second suicide was mine. Sure, it sounds ridiculous! I am still able to walk and breathe. I play with my son and his friends from P.S. 122 and P.S. 20 and take them to the movies. I walk my new dog, Igor, to the East River Park or Tompkins Square Park, or play with her in our backyard. I still drink beer and play chess. I am still doing my pen-and-inks and piano constructions, although I haven't seen a piano thrown out on the streets for sometime now. A few things have happened to me since that famous spring of 1969, and a few things are still happening. I've made a movie about the old Slavic people in the East Village. I've sat in the famous Tombs. Well, a few things, at least. So I live. Or do I? Whatever, I did commit suicide after my show at Contact. And when they took me to good old Bernstein Institute, I was already dead. Now I am working hard at resurrection. It's like swimming upstream. Resurrections only happen in legends.

I did not want to commit suicide. Things were going badly for me, but I was somehow surviving, hanging by my teeth and slowly pulling myself together. I think I'd have been O.K. if I could only have gotten out of the city for a few weeks. Just to the seashore somewhere or to a forest.

No such luck!

Instead, I happened to meet that gigantic jellyfish of American life whose tentacles reached even beyond Avenue B into the land of the Apes (or Dogs). The Great American Psychotherapy Machine with all its bullshit and all its Thorazines and Tofranils, Stellazines and Libriums, electric-shock treatments—oh, yes, they're alive and well—psychodrama and group therapy, padded cells and barred windows.

That jellyfish has quite a sting.

I was stung.
But it's all in the past.
The end does come to everything.
Even to suburban supermarkets and drive-in movies.
There must be a field of wheat somewhere. I want to roll in it so bad, watch the sky and the sparrows.

Once There Was a Village

Visit No. 2 from Psychiatrist No. 1.

In my studio, a railroad flat cluttered with constructions and sculptures, cans of paints and brushes on the bathtub and a homemade table, two easels, and an old drafting table with a pile of small piano pieces on top of it, an almost-finished piano-construction sitting on two chairs. Further in, a large loft bed and clothing thrown on the floor. It's more chaotic than usual because early in the evening, about a half-hour prior to this visit, an attempt was made to steal some of my constructions. To steal anything. The junkie actually got inside my studio by lowering himself on a rope from the roof. He was discovered and chased to a balcony which was a part of an old fire escape, from which he jumped two floors down to the backyard and was further chased by everybody through the snow and the slush. Several bricks and a hammer were thrown after him, but the junkie escaped with only a slight limp. A few minutes before the visit, I managed to clean up the junkie's vomit and most of the things thrown around the studio. My thoughts were quite disjointed at the moment. And it was cold; one of my windows had been busted in the process.

NO. 1:   Hi, Yuri, good to see you, man, how are you tonight?

ME: O.K., I guess.

NO. 1:   (Looks penetrating, waits for me to continue)

ME: You know, I've been thinking. Maybe I should get out of here. I mean out of the city for a while. I am not doing anybody any good here, that's for sure. Get some fresh air like I used to do before I had my coffeehouse. When things got too heavy, I'd drive south for a few days or even a week. That's how I started writing. I was working this straight job for over three years after I got out of the Army, and I split up with my first wife. Speaking about changes, I was really going through the changes then. I didn't have any vacation days coming; I just drove down to Virginia, and before I knew it, I was in Georgia. Then I had four flat tires, wound up in Gainesville, Florida. I was so tired and the weather was rotten, snow and sleet all the way. I took this room in a tourist home and when I woke up, everything was different. The whole life was different! Sunshine was pouring into my room, birds were singing outside, and there were two large palms growing by my window. Before that, I'd never even seen a real palm. Everything was so new and fresh. I felt so good. I wrote a couple of poems. Stupid poems, about children playing in the sun and lost love. And when I was driving back through the Okefenokee Swamp, I wrote some more poems. When I opened my coffeehouse, Unicorn, I used to do the same thing. Whenever pressure built up, I'd jump in the car and DRIVE! By that time, I was married again and my wife used to call my boss—I was working two jobs then——and tell him I was deathly ill. And I'd be driving through the West Virginia mountains.

NO. 1: I think your leaving everything and going out for a drive is nothing more than escaping reality. Don't you realize that? I mean, why can't you deal with what's happening? There's nothing to be afraid of. Nothing to be ashamed of. There's absolutely no reason for running away.

ME: And when we lived in San Francisco, after I got rid of the coffeehouse, I used to drive alone to Placerville and the Great Reservoir area. I remember once I slept on a tiny island on the American River. It was so quiet, you wouldn't believe. Tiny, tiny sounds of water and cows wandering around with their bells.

NO. 1: Life, unfortunately, is not something you can escape from. You do have certain responsibilities and until you learn to deal with these responsibilities, you'll never be truly at peace with yourself.

ME: Look at it this way. YOU'VE had your vacation. YOU told me you just returned from your vacation. I've been living here five fucking years now, and living here is no joke. I've worked all kinds of jobs and collected unemployment a few times and painted my ass off and made my movies, and even did some writing. The only time I got out of here was when I was working for Benton No-Balls and I took my family to Expo '67. I haven't even seen clean air for at least five years.

NO. 1: Look at him now, he sounds like a little child. Would you like to cry about it, would you like to climb into your mother's womb?

ME: I'd consider anything now. Hang on a minute. When I said I worked, I mean it may not seem like work to you. I'm not going to get any college degrees for it, I can't put what I did on résumés. Like what you see now, this construction, I've worked on it for three days and three nights in a row. You have to glue every little piece and not just anywhere. You have to get just the right feeling for movement, that's before I even start painting it. Like tonight, I'll work on it long after you're asleep.

NO. 1:   There's no reason to feel sorry for yourself. That's what I am trying to say. You're a productive artist. You don't have to sell me. I see it every time I come over here. You've lived a full life. [Pause] Perhaps too full. You should be able to transcend this feeling of being trapped and persecuted.

ME: I don't feel persecuted at all. But I am trapped. I tell you, I am trapped! I can't get out even if I had a car and some money. I'd be worried sick about my wife and my kid. I know it's hard for you to comprehend, but try—our block is very dangerous right now. How long do you think it would take our ripoffs to figure out I'm gone and my wife works and my son goes to school and my dog is small?

NO. 1:   Yes, I know, it's terrible. It's getting to be unsafe everywhere. [No. 1 lives somewhere on Long Island and comes to counsel the drug-users and flipouts around here once a week.] Crime, riots, sometimes I think this whole society is falling apart . . .

ME: Take last night. My neighbors were returning home and all four of them were taken off downstairs in our hallway. One chick did scream, but by the time me and Louie ran out, they were long gone. And we couldn't do anything, besides; they had guns.

NO. 1:   [Continuing] I say running away solves

	nothing. Besides, as you pointed out, it might well endanger your wife and son. Let's change the subject for the few minutes we've left. You mentioned last week you'd met another woman. Do you wish to tell me about her?
ME:	She's very nice, she's an artist too.
NO. 1:	Did you take her to bed yet?
ME:	A couple of times.
NO. 1:	Well now, that's news. Did you enjoy it?
ME:	Sure.
NO. 1:	What about her?
ME:	I think she did too. I certainly hope so.
NO. 1:	Are you sure you're going to have that show at Contact?
ME:	I am sure now. I spoke to Larry and he said fine. Probably next week, maybe in a couple of weeks, but it's definite now.
NO. 1:	I am happy for you! I think that's a very good beginning. [Consults his watch.] I think that's what you need. What is your relationship with your wife?
ME:	My wife doesn't speak to me right now, we had another fight.
NO. 1:	Did you hit her?
ME:	I don't hit her any more . . . she threw scissors at me.
NO. 1:	And missed?
ME:	Almost.
NO. 1:	The two of you are so intense, I've never seen any couple who go to such extremes as you, and so often. One day you seem to get along so well and the next day, boom!
ME:	We are a high-strung family.

[Sounds of police sirens outside. Popping noises, such as firecrackers, cherry bombs, or shots. People yelling in the street. No. 1 is getting a little uneasy.]

NO. 1: Could you come next week to my office?
ME: All right.
NO. 1: Only don't forget to show up, Thursday,
         five thirty sharp.
ME: Sure, sure.

Tompkins Square Park on a lovely spring afternoon. Old
Slavic people sit and stand around soaking up the sun.
Puerto Rican and black kids are playing basketball or hand-
ball; the Ukrainian kids are playing hockey. The hippies are
crowded by the band shell with their dogs. Lots of people
are playing checkers or chess. A few guitars are strumming;
bongo drums. I am sitting at one of the chess tables playing
with Psychiatrist No. 3, a hippie-looking man with a long
reddish beard. No. 3 is a good friend; we've known each
other for years. What's more important, he's a good chess-
player. We have great respect for one another. No. 3 is also
going through hoops. He's decided to quit his profession
and is organizing a commune on one of the islands in
Minnesota. It's a beautiful, beautiful day, unusually warm.

ME: You wouldn't believe it—but I've been
         seeing a shrink these past few months.
NO. 3: Watch your queen, Yuri, put it there
         again and I will grab her.
ME: I just wanted your professional opinion.
NO. 3: You're full of shit.
ME: Look, I really have troubles. Lots of
         troubles.
NO. 3: You think I don't have troubles?
ME: You told me yourself, you had to go
         through years of analysis and now you're
         balanced and all that shit.
NO. 3: Yuri, listen, there's day and there's night,
         there's summer and there's winter,

Once There Was a Village

there's real life and there's bullshit. Now, what are we talking about?

ME: You don't think it'll do me any good?

NO. 3:   No way! And do you want to know why?

ME: Why?

NO. 3:   Because you're a creative man and the science of psychiatry, if it is a science, as it now exists is not prepared to deal with any creative person. You wanted my professional opinion? O.K.—you cut this shit out because you're going to get fucked through and through.

ME: Look, I can deal with anything, you've been to my coffeehouse and you know all the shit I had to put up with. But now, what's happening with my family, you know when I think about my wife and my son, I haven't even been able to sleep these past few weeks. I have these weird nightmares. You know, we were so close. I wake up and I'm covered with cold sweat. Look at me, I'm a wreck.

NO. 3:   O.K. Let me prescribe some sleeping pills for you. If you feel any worse, come on over to my place and I'll give you some Librium. Only I don't believe in any of these tranquilizers. I've seen too many normal people reduced to zombies.

ME: Give me your sleeping pills. Maybe you've got something to help me stop drinking so much?

NO. 3:   I'll give you some Librium. Take it for a week and then we'll see. What's your shrink think?

ME: I don't really know. He's a strange guy, he's got these purple wings.

NO. 3:   You keep on drinking all that beer and

		you'll grow purple wings yourself. Check your queen.
ME:		When are you leaving?
NO.	3:	[Hopefully] Around the first of May.
ME:		You've made your first mistake.
NO.	3:	Just make your move . . . You know, O.K., you and your wife love each other, but can't live with one another and your son is a great kid. And both of you love him and he loves you. Now take my miserable situation—my wife is a motherfuckin' bitch. At least yours isn't a bitch, that's a very big difference. And both my sons have very serious psychological problems. Not the kind of shit you're running around and yelling about, but real deep problems. And my bitch aggravates these problems every single day. The guy she lives with right now is a criminally insane sadist. He beats her up and even tortures her, which is all right with me, and she loves it, but recently he started beating up my kids.
ME:		So, what are you going to do?
NO.	3:	I am going to keep cool this month because I am going to kill both of them before I split and take the kids with me to my island.
ME:		You're nuts. You're the one who needs help.
NO.	3:	Yuri, am I such a bad chess-player? Check, by the way. I'll get away with it, don't you worry.

No. 3 got away with it, from what I heard, and in style. He is now living where the air is fresh with his two sons, his new wife, their three-year-old daughter, and a two-year-old Indian girl they've adopted. I received a postcard from him once. He's working as a carpenter. He built his own house. He said he missed our games. I miss him, too. He's the only man I know, aside from Jimmy Richardson, with whom I've never played a mediocre game of chess.

Call No. 2 to Psychiatrist No. 2

Hello, no, this is the doctor's answering service. Transfers, etc.

NO. 2: This is————. [Hospital noises in background.]

ME: Look, something just isn't working out.

NO. 2: What?

ME: I don't know, that's just it. I am getting more and more depressed.

NO. 2: You're still considering suicide?

ME: I am thinking about many things. Mostly about how useless I've suddenly become. I need something to cheer me up fast. No. I wouldn't give me anything. Maybe you can give me something?

NO. 2: Like what?

ME: Like something to make me happier.

NO. 2: What you want is the proverbial pill of happiness. I am sorry, we haven't discovered it yet. I am not even allowed to prescribe acid. Hmm, try Tofranil. You're not going to feel better right away, it'll take about three days to build up. I'll call the Avenue D pharmacy.

ME: Thanks, I really appreciate it.

NO. 2: Only you can't drink so much when you're on it.

ME: I'll cut down.

NO. 2: If you feel any worse, call me immediately. Why don't you come and see me, anyway? What about this Saturday, around four?

ME: O.K.

NO. 2:   Remember, if anything comes up, call me
          immediately.
ME: All right, I will.

SLOWLY, EVER SO SLOWLY.

I am coming out of the Thorazine void. Thoughts of love, hate, unclear. A lifeboat in search of a shore. Very fine milky fog. The distant noise of breakers. An unexplored continent somewhere just beyond the reefs. Sunshine. Tall, soft grass. Silence in the majestic Redwood Forest. A portfolio of bright, cheerful watercolors. Soon, very soon. Almost there. And just like Rousseau's snake-charmer, it all trembles and is beginning to fade. Grayer and grayer grows the realization. Until the snake-charmer himself leaves his small canvas, until the watercolors turn into gloomy ikons and I am aware of the rain.

The rain and the wind. Both angry, determined, penetrating. A horde of German tourists invades the corner café. I get up from my bench and button my raincoat. Only a sailor and his girl remain upon their bench under the chestnuts. A sailor and his girl. Always.

I stop for a moment to buy a postcard. The one with the sunset over the River Seine and the Eiffel Tower, the prettiest one. No, I am not going to buy the set of postcards with seventy-two positions. I've had enough positions already. I am ordering a beer, I am looking at the Rue Dauphine. French beer isn't so bad after the first two glasses. I said I'd be back around one. It's two now, and it looks like the rain might stop. She couldn't sleep all night. She said she wanted so much to wake me up, but I was out of it. She took a couple of her tranquilizers and felt groggy in the morning. Her eyes were puffed up and reddish. Her very light hazel eyes, almost golden. So unusual for a Japanese.

Another beer, another year. Chrysanthemums are growing all over Paris, it seems. Around the statues and the monuments. When my grandmother died, the year the war began, my mother and I planted chrysanthemums on her grave. I remember that grave so well, I used to go and talk

Once There Was a Village

to my grandmother often. And I remember the old wooden church and the beggars. And how we were dying from hunger and catching rats. And how we tried saving our burning house during the bombing. And the day the Germans took our city, and another day when they started taking our people and locking them into the boxcars.

The German tourists are happy now. They're exuding health and wealth; they're the conquerors after all.

Another beer, and I am going back to the room with the strawberry wallpaper. I want to stroke the long, black hair and kiss the hazel eyes, almost golden.

We do not have any political prisoners in our American mental institutions. Russia, sure, as everyone knows. Read Tarsis's *Ward 7*, for example. To me, that book rang a bit false but it has its moments. A question, then; why are there so many talented, creative people in American mental institutions? In good old Bernstein, on the seventh floor, in a relatively small ward, there were three composers, three writers, two artists (I am counting myself as an artist), three musicians, one singer, two actresses, one actor, an architect, a dancer, and a fashion designer.

At least half the ward's population were creative people. And really creative people, not the phoney baloney I met when I was working in advertising agencies. In many ways, Bernstein is not a typical place. So, I've talked to a few survivors of other mental institutions. They all insist on one thing: at least a third of the patients in their wards were creative people. I can't say that I don't see what I see —American mental institutions are also jails, in some ways even more dangerous than Attica or San Quentin. Ever heard of anybody coming out of an institution, like Central Islip, after being there six or seven years?

The American mental wards are the keepers of a tremendous, highly-dangerous-to-the-System, creative force that is wasted, zapped by Thorazine, etc., and slowly killed off.

The concept of creativity on the outside boils down to

this: If you're so talented, how come you're not rich or famous? Yet reality works on exactly the opposite premise. The more talent you have, the less your chance of making it. Meaning mostly lots of money and prestige. Because the System does not need creative people. Far from it, it barely survives on mediocrity. The last thing it needs is somebody doing something new. And the few talented artists who "made it" also happened to be very talented hustlers. That's where the dog lies buried. To function within this society, and maybe have a little dignity, the artist must grow two heads: one with which to create and the other to sell. Of course, there are rich wives, parents, girlfriends, boyfriends, certain cliques that have access to commercial galleries or foundation grants—all that, or part of it, helps. But if you don't have it, forget it! Forget your talent, your art; throw your easel out of the window and get a job in a supermarket or start driving a cab. Like I am doing right now.

And if you persist in creating your thing—paintings, constructions, whatever (unless, of course, you're doing plastic and polyester sculptures that actually fuck and you can rig their motors so that the fucking will be synchronized with what you have on your stereo set—Stones, Dylan, Melanie, Cat Stevens, etc.), be careful. Very soon you'll be starving slowly and being isolated. "Where did all my friends go?" And you *will* be isolated, baby, especially if you're trying to say something important. And, above all, be prepared to visit such exotic places as Bellevue, St. Luke's, Central Islip, Bernstein, and thousands of others, large and small, where your thinking will be straightened out, OH YEAH OR ELSE! It'll be so straight you won't even be able to cut a corner.

Well, I, too, can appreciate the new checkered linoleum on the floor and long corridors leading nowhere. And the times when the gorgeous red-haired nurse would come to my coffinlike room and say, "Now open your mouth, Yuri, and please swallow. Now stick out your tongue. Thank you."

It was important to open my mouth and stick out my tongue because they thought I was hiding my horsecaps of Thorazine and later flushing them down the drain like any normal patient. Actually, I was honest, at first, and was taking my "medications." Only after my vision blurred, along with my thinking, I realized I'd better stop, or else I'd be there forever.

Sometimes I'd get back at the nurses by pretending I am Count Dracula and just as she'd peer into my mouth, I'd let out a bloodcurdling scream, raise my beard, and flap my wings, and she'd usually howl too and drop her tray with medications.

There was, however, this padded cell, and the head nurse, a very nice lady, put it to me in plain English. "Any more shit like that and you go to the padded cell with THE KID."

The Kid was a totally flipped-out hippie they dug up somewhere on St. Marks and brought here along with his one hundred thousand lice. An official oversight—these lice not only jumped upon the patients and the nurses in our ward but also walked downstairs to the addict population, to the doctors and their briefcases, to the guards, everywhere, everybody was itching. I am still itching just thinking about it. I loaned that Kid a pair of my pants—his own pants were held by seven or eight safety pins and it was very painful to watch him get out of the bathroom and try to close them; they were his zipper. The Kid never gave me back my pants. I think one day he walked out of the hospital and the guards were too astounded to stop him in time. And everybody was relieved.

I did a couple of other sneaky things, I admit it. On my third day there, I stole a pair of wire-cutters they used in Occupational Therapy to cut copper sheets for ceramic jewelry. I was going to cut through the thick wire mesh on my window—installed there for precisely such a possibility and checked by the nurses periodically—and make a splash, as it were. To climb on the ledge and cry out something like, "Watch me, motherfuckers, I can fly, I can fly!" and fly down on top of some Second Avenue bus. Psychiatrist No. 2 talked me out of it in one of our heavier conversations. I gave back the wire-cutters.

The second thing I am not going to divulge—some poor soul might need that avenue of escape some day, and if he's as desperate as I was, he'll think of it too.

By that time, I was under constant observation anyway and couldn't do much with the male nurse sitting by my bed day and night. And in a few days I wasn't interested in killing myself as much as in getting the hell out of there.

I became a very reasonable man from that time on to my first, and I might add, my only weekend pass.

During my second week, I developed an unusual problem. I couldn't sleep. I just couldn't. A whole week went by, I counted all the days and nights and even the hours. I didn't get one minute's sleep. All the Thorazine and all the other crap they were feeding me couldn't even make me yawn. I'd been promised that this capsule or that pill would surely put me to sleep and this one would definitely knock me out because it was THE knockout pill. Nothing doing.

Night after night I lay awake with my mind racing wildly, combing my entire life, until morning. That's when the construction workers would begin drilling their holes across the street. I couldn't sleep during the day, I couldn't sleep in the evening. Eventually, they gave me a thing called "green jelly bean" and told me I could have another one at two in the morning. That "green jelly bean" produced the weirdest reaction—I was swimming in my own sweat, my bed sheets were soaked, and the rushes and some kind of humming sound almost put me to sleep. At two in the morning, I stumbled to the nurses' station next door to my room and took another jelly bean. I shouldn't have done it.

Immediately, the humming grew in pitch and changed into very clear distant singing. The songs were all Russian in origin. They were a mixture of prayers, folk songs, and revolutionary marches, sometimes all combined into one. And visually, I saw in the padded cell on the other side of the nurses' station an old Russian man on his knees. He was crossing himself fervently and crying for forgiveness of his sins to the all-merciful Jesus Christ and Saint Seraphim of Sarov. This man touched me so much, I felt I must talk with him in the morning. I just had to! I knew he couldn't communicate with anyone else, and I knew he'd been in that padded cell a very long time because they'd all forgotten about him.

Somehow, I knew exactly what the old man wanted to say and how he felt. As if his prayers and penance were first coming THROUGH ME. I didn't want to sleep now, the whole thing felt very pleasurable, very sexual. In the morning I had quite a shock—as soon as I entered the washroom, the singing began again. Much stronger than at night. Now I could also see the people who were singing, hundreds and hundreds of them. And behind that huge chorus, on a hill, dressed in flaming red robes and tied to some hideous wooden object, was my old man. Now he was shaking his chains and screaming curses and accusations AT ME. And I thought, "Man, I don't even know you." It wasn't pleasurable any more, I was scared.

I stood under an ice-cold shower for as long as I could stand it. I tried pinching myself, squeezing my balls, and pressing my eardrums. But since the chorus was situated inside my forehead and the old man was sitting even deeper in my head, there was nothing I could do, except cry. "Now you've really had it, Yuri," was all I could think of. "Now you've finally flipped."

I was afraid to open my mouth.

After breakfast I decided I had nothing to lose, so I might as well start pulling myself together. This was ridiculous! I had never flown so high on anything. And I've been to parties where the punch was so spiked some of the guests are still in Rockland Mental Hospital. This couldn't last, I kept telling myself. And, sure enough, a few hours later I realized that this crazy hallucination is strongest when I'm in an enclosed area, such as a bathroom, or my tiny room, or when I'm standing next to walls. This was quite a relief. The hallucinations lasted about three days, getting weaker and weaker. And I did get some sleep.

Back in the land of the Apes, just before entering Bernstein, I had finished two large pieces of artwork. One was my biggest piano construction—a four-foot by eight-foot sheet of three-quarter-inch plywood covered by hundreds, if not thousands, of small wooden piano parts. Several movements, designs, and four or five layers all interwoven into something resembling rivers and islands, or possibly cities. I don't know; everyone who saw it interpreted it differently. I painted the whole thing reddish brown, almost burnt umber and almost in monotone. I think it's my best piano construction by far. In terms of time alone, it took me a couple of months working every night and day to finish it. I've exhibited it at the Educational Alliance and just recently in our East Village group show, also at the Educational Alliance.

The second piece was a six-foot by five-foot seascape, actually a painting of a huge wave cresting. I did it in my usual seascape technique—with a palette knife and layers upon layers of oil paint. It, too, was quite a painting. I really don't know what to think of it. It turned out to be more realistic than I expected; very few people wanted to sit under it. It hung at Contact for a while, freaking out the freaks. The last time I saw it, it was hanging at a place called The Blue Guerrilla up in Harlem, on 125th Street near Fifth Avenue.

I thought about these two pieces when I was walking back home from Bernstein. Walking, excuse me, to a place which I still loved but which I felt was no longer my home.

That was the strangest walk in my entire life. It was about seven in the morning, on Saturday morning, when I signed

76   *Once There Was a Village*

out and received my brown envelope with "medications." The large elevator was going down so slowly, it probably took me half an hour to get to the ground floor.

Yes, this time I did have a pass and I showed it to the guards. They were nice guys, both of them. They were more interested in looking over the pen-and-inks I was carrying home with me. I was in no hurry, and we rapped a while. The Puerto Rican guard was taking oil painting at the New School. He told me he saw plenty of art while he was stationed in Germany, but never anything like my pen-and-inks. He thought they were good. The black guy thought they were good, too, even asked me about the price. I felt flattered. Didn't want to leave.

It was a hot New York morning, and the air-pollution level must have been terrible. If I had taken off my cap and hung it in the air, it would never have fallen to the ground.

Busy Second Avenue was empty, no traffic at all. I was sleepwalking until I got to the fruit stands on First Avenue and heard the first sounds of life. From there, each step closer felt like a step further. I almost could not lift my feet.

I met a few people I knew, said something to them, and they said something to me.

Before going into my house, I stopped to look at Contact's door. There was a small note taped to it:

"Psychiatric Counseling.

The Shrink will be here on Thursdays, 9-11 P.M."

Under it was a poster with a needle: "Speed Kills." A few guys were drinking wine and laughing away the time on the corner of Seventh and C.

A garbage truck was coming my way.

"The end comes to everything, the end has to be accepted," I kept telling myself, yet some endings a man cannot accept, no matter what. Or put out of his mind. What a powerful thing human memory is, and what a dangerous thing too.

In the hallway, the mosquitoes began biting me. I heard my dog barking upstairs. She knew I was coming back. I didn't know it, but she knew.

Eagerly and reluctantly. Very reluctantly.

Second floor, third floor, fourth floor, stop.

Knock.

Once There Was a Village

The rest of the year things were quieter on our block. One Albanian woman was assaulted and the Albanians later shot and killed the man who had done it. There were still many ripoffs and stabbings, but not nearly as many as in '69. I guess we'd reached the saturation point and the majority of junkies had moved on to greener pastures. There were more Albanians moving in and more Puerto Ricans moving out. The bohemian population remained approximately the same. The chick next door took off for Hawaii along with her whole therapy group. A young actor moved in.

And just a couple of months after I came back, the quiet death began paying attention to our quiet house once again.

This time it was the fat Irishman on the second floor. He was not a pleasant man, far from it. Soon after they moved in, I had a big fight with him. I had a knife, he a baseball bat. The grandmother finally separated us. I wasn't the only one who fought with him. This guy hated everybody—"Fascist-Communist cocksuckers" was one of his milder descriptions of our hippie types. I can't even mention what he called the blacks and the Puerto Ricans. And the Slavs weren't far behind. In fact, he was even more insulting to Slavs. He had a daily fight going with the grandmother and his sons, and also with Mike, who, at first, was dismayed by his new neighbor, and with Mike's sister. What he called Mike also shouldn't be printed. He was not a pleasant guy and yet I remember him with fondness. He was always hanging out of the window and knew absolutely EVERYTHING that went on on our block. After a year or so of living here, he began to mellow considerably. He wouldn't yell at the kids all the time. Sometimes he'd even come down and buy a bottle or two of Pedro Domeq brandy which he'd share with a few Puerto Rican men from the next building. On one such occasion, I was coming home very late and he even asked me to join them. And we drank until early in the morning. He could drink, too. Not nearly as much as Mike, but he could drink. What he couldn't do was sleep nights. He had all kinds of sleeping pills and tranquilizers but they didn't help much. So, whenever he wasn't hanging out of the window, or yelling at someone, he'd sit with Mike in Mike's apartment and talk while Mike finished his third quart of whiskey. He bought a car twice. Both times he had bad luck: Once the engine cracked, and the other time somebody slammed into him somewhere near Baltimore and almost killed him and his older son. He was a gambler, too. Once he showed me a roll of bills in his pocket, I almost died. There must have been at least a couple of thousand dollars in that roll. He must have had the luck of the Irish, at least sometimes. He was always lecturing Mike on the evils of alcohol and how Mike was killing himself. I guess it never occurred to him that he might go first.

Just before he died, he became even more irritable again, more than ever. He began to have fights with Mike over any small thing. And Mike had had it. He told me he'd stopped talking to that Irish ———. Mike could swear eloquently, too. I thought they'd be friends again, more or less, in a few days as usual, but no. This time something must have really happened because Mike didn't talk to the Irishman any more. And in a couple of weeks, the Irish guy died. It was a surprise to everyone because all of us in the house thought Mike would be the first to go.

Ever since we had moved into the building, we'd been good friends with the Carpatho-Russian lady, Dora, who later became our super. She was the one who kept our house clean. For some reason, she mopped the halls just before daybreak EVERY Saturday morning. She also kept the backyard clean, not an easy thing to do. And she kept our coal stove going.

She'd worked on farms and she'd worked in New York sweatshops and factories. She had known real oppression. She had seen it all and then some. From the time she was twelve, she had worked ten hours a day, six and a half days a week, packing boxes for a clothing manufacturer right here on the Lower East Side. She went to work on the farms in New Jersey, and that was no picnic. When we met her, her

Once There Was a Village

husband was dead. She had a married daughter in Jamaica, Queens. And she was sharing the apartment with Freddy the super. They did not bother one another much and got along. She was always a very composed woman and had a quiet dignity about her that's difficult to describe. She was a great person.

She was friendly with every other Slavic lady on the block and in the neighborhood. She was not all that religious, but occasionally she'd go to a tiny forgotten Russian church on Fourth Street near Avenue D, or to the Russian cathedral on Second Street. She loved to take out her old chair and sit on our stoop for hours. Sometimes she'd get together with the old Slavic women from across the street, and they'd all sit and chat in the sun.

She also loved to get out to Tompkins Square Park. One evening, we were sitting on the stoop and she came back from the park looking very happy. They'd had a concert of Latin, Slavic, and soul music in the park, and out of all the performers, she'd loved the steel band the best.

She was an understanding woman. Once, when my wife and I had a terrific fight, she became very concerned. She figured that if she could hear us all the way down from the fourth floor, it must be serious. She got the Polish lady from the third floor, who was also concerned, and they both came up to my floor. They were going to knock but decided not to. They chickened out, as she later told me. Anyway, our fight was over just about then.

She was also very good to our son, and when my two daughters from my first marriage spent a few months with us, she accepted them with touching tenderness. And when I had a show of my piano constructions and other wild constructions at Contact, she was one of the first to come. She really took her time looking everything over. And she was a good critic, too. She liked my round piano construction called "The War Is Not Yet Over." She also liked my Allbrau beer-bottle-cap-and-broken-beer-bottle construction, which I called "Homage To The Unknown Brand," and she liked my broken-glass-and-charred-wood construction called "On Avenue C." Incidentally, these were the only pieces out of some seventy I've exhibited which were titled. Maybe she could identify more with a piece of work that had a definite meaning. She also liked my realistic pen-and-ink seascapes, and she told me that although she liked the sea, she rarely went to the beach.

The thing that amazed me about Dora was her tolerance of everyone—that, coming from a person whom the American intolerance, bigotry, and greed tried to beat into the ground for so many years. She used to say, "Puerto Ricans, they are good people." About the hippies, her opinion was, "Poor babies, they want fathers and mothers." She told me once that she wouldn't mind adopting one hippie chick who was a speed-freak and a junkie and was hustling up and down Avenue C, because "she is a good child inside." She had a high opinion of blacks in general and especially of them as workers, something with which most Slavic workers grudgingly agree. She told me she'd worked with blacks in the fields and in the factories and had many black friends. She was the one who had most tolerance for Mike and his drinking: "Poor man knows exactly what he is doing and only God can stop him." She had a wonderful sense of humor—and two boyfriends. One was a Ukrainian; the other was the old Spanish man on the top floor.

For a few months we had noticed she was beginning to lose weight rapidly. She was literally melting before our eyes. She also became weaker and even let the stove go out a few times. And she stopped mopping the floors. Her daughter decided that enough was enough. One evening she came with her husband and took Dora, almost by force, to their home in Jamaica. They left us the keys to her apartment and told us that we could have anything we wanted from it. My wife refused to go down. I went, prompted by my morbid curiosity. The apartment was filled with an incredible amount of things collected over years and years of hard life. For instance, she had a large shopping bag full of wooden clothespins that must have fallen off our clotheslines over the past twenty years. And she had cans of

Once There Was a Village

surplus food that had rusted solidly on the outside. There were the usual paper ikons on her bureau, all neatly arranged, and an ancient Russian book on how to interpret dreams, which I took. I also took four shot-glasses that were standing next to the empty vodka bottle I gave her for Christmas.

Mike was just getting over one of his binges at that time, and I let him into her apartment. He picked up a bunch of old pots and pans and some surplus food.

Dora's daughter called us a few times afterward—she was afraid Dora's Social Security checks might get lost or stolen. Dora was in the hospital by that time. No one thought she'd die; she just wasn't the type. But she died. From cancer. She was also at Jarema's funeral parlor, but I didn't have the heart to go and see her there. I know she'll forgive me.

Just a short time later, I was walking home one morning and met our new super taking his dog to the park. We exchanged the usual greetings. As I walked away, he suddenly turned around and almost shouted, "Yuri, did you know Mike died last night?"

It was a beautiful morning and our block seemed unusually clean. A few kids were playing basketball in the playground and some dogs ran back and forth. Beer trucks were delivering beer. A tiny Slavic kid, incredibly fucked up in the head, was trying to set fire to the synagogue. I took away his matches and pushed him away. But I guess it wasn't enough; the synagogue burned down later in the afternoon.

No, I didn't know Mike had died.

I'd just seen Mike the other day through his slightly opened door. He was talking with one of his nephews. He looked weak and pale, but I'd seen him looking worse. He seemed relatively sober; I guessed he was coming out of his binge. Mike always called me "Yurik," a tender Russian diminutive. I thought I'd stop by later on and take back our dishes and make him some more soup.

Mike! Mike! Mike!

Too many memories are so very much alive. As I sat in

Tompkins Square Park a couple of days later trying to shake a hangover, an old drinking buddy of Mike's came over. He said, "Yuri, Mike's at Jarema's. You'd better hurry up, he'll be buried tomorrow." I just looked at the guy and didn't say anything and he limped away. I wasn't about to even go past Jarema's any more.

That night I REALLY got drunk. Again. I was observing the great Russian tradition of drinking for the well-being of the departed soul. I hoped God, if he existed, would take good care of Mike's soul. I was also drinking for the souls of thousands of other Mikes and Doras and Bills who were so cruelly fucked up by America, the beautiful. And for thousands and thousands more who are still living on about a hundred bucks or less a month in the ratholes of the East Village.

The real East Village, east of Avenue B. Who are being ripped off by the junkies and spat upon by the pigs. Who have only enough money for one decent meal a week. About whom nothing was ever written in the New York *Times* or the *Village Voice* and never will be.

I think these great people deserve much better. They worked so hard and they got nothing. I don't think it would cost our government that much to get them out of the slums they live in and buy them a few villages somewhere in New Jersey or Pennsylvania. Someplace where they could open their windows and see the sunflowers growing and hear the birds sing. Where they could relax and take a walk outside in the evening to look at the clear sky and stars. Where they could BREATHE their last days and hours.

God, they've earned it!

Now, except for the Spanish man on the top floor, we are the oldest tenants in the building. We've lived here about five years and it feels like five lifetimes.

A young Puerto Rican couple with a tiny baby and a black Great Dane, good friends of ours from the old block, are moving into Mike's apartment.

And it's another summer.

Once There Was a Village

In many good Russian novels, the author addresses the reader directly from time to time.

Something like: "Dear Reader: In the years that have flown . . ."

I find this endearing and personal and I am going to use this approach to try and answer to myself, as well as to you, my good mysterious Reader, why I am still doing piano constructions and why I am writing this book which is Russian all right, but I wouldn't exactly call it a novel. First, about my constructions.

Dear Reader, I was walking home one winter night in 1966. My teeth were chattering, my ass was half-frozen. There was lots of snow and ice on the ground. I am one Russian who really hates cold weather. I nearly froze to death as a kid during the war and I still remember it. That night, I was also a little bit high.

On Sixth Street between Avenues A and B, closer to A, I stumbled on some thrown-out objects and fell, slightly injuring my knee and my head. The objects I fell upon were parts of an old piano thrown all across the sidewalk. The keys, boards, wires, and so on. I got up, looked around —one bunch was neatly tied together—and they were beautiful white keys. I picked them up and took them to my studio. Later that night, I came back and picked up the rest of the piano pieces. I put them in a corner of my studio and they remained there for a few weeks. At the time, I was at the crossroads, creatively speaking. I was painting realistic portraits and nudes, and I was still doing my pen-and-inks. Also, I had just finished a period of painting abstract designs on pieces of wood. I hadn't done any constructions yet.

I had this large half of a round tabletop sitting by the wall, not far from the piano pieces. One evening, I took the old shellac off my tabletop and was getting ready to paint some design on it when an idea hit me: Why not use the piano keys, arrange them like sunrays on the tabletop, and get a three-dimensional effect of a rising sun? Very simple, I almost did it as a joke. I glued every piece together, put hooks and wires in back, and hung it up. It looked better than I'd expected. I still like that piece every time I see it and the person who has it likes it very much.

From there it was easy for me to see the infinite possibilities of piano constructions.

With every construction, I was learning something new. The constructions themselves were becoming more and more exciting to me and, obviously, to the people who bought them. I also did quite a few other constructions using practically every material I could lay my hands on, but none of the things could come even close to piano pieces—there's something very spiritual about piano keys, small keys especially.

I didn't give up my pen-and-inks. I don't think I could ever give them up. My wife was only half-kidding when she said once to somebody, "The world would be ending, the city sinking into the Bay"—we were in San Francisco—"and Yuri would still be sitting doing a pen-and-ink seascape."

And I didn't give up any of the other things I do from time to time.

Yet the piano constructions have greatly enriched my whole creative life. They continue to enrich it now. I have not the slightest desire to stop doing them. Only a week ago I took down my show at the Educational Alliance. I made smaller piano constructions last year, but I was doing something new with them and I was proud of every one of them.

Over the years, I have found over fifty thrown-out pianos on the streets of the Lower East Side. These were pianos, parts of which I was able to use. The Educational Alliance, the good people that they are, gave me four of the pianos which they were replacing and, I believe, will give me another two soon. When University of the Streets was throwing away its old pianos, I was there to pick them up. When Tompkins Square Community Center was in operation, I got the insides of one of their broken pianos. A concert pianist who bought one of my pen-and-inks is giving me one of his old pianos. The Frog Pond, a bar where I

Once There Was a Village

worked part-time as a bartender, promised me their broken piano—it costs too much to tune and fix it. And all my friends would tip me off immediately about any piano that might be thrown out.

Chances are, Dear Reader, that you'll never see my piano constructions in any museum. Then why go on?

For myself, for people. Ordinary people. Over three hundred of whom, from many walks of life, have my works hanging or standing in their apartments, storefronts, lofts, and houses.

From time to time, I receive a letter from somebody saying roughly, "Yuri, we just wanted to tell you how much we enjoy your seascape, how proud we are to have it . . ." Some people even send me slides of my works on their walls. And I feel good.

And it all becomes worthwhile. I go on and do another construction, another pen-and-ink. I think to myself: Long after I am dead and forgotten, parts of me, my works, will continue making life a little bit more pleasant for these people, their families and their friends. And again, I feel proud.

This is not an ego trip, but simply the pride of a hard-working person. And my feelings toward my art are probably similar to those of a farmer toward his fields, or a bricklayer looking at a house he's just built. It's a part of my life, that's all.

And now, why am I writing this book? Again, for myself, for people. Slavic people in particular. I had to write it because my feelings toward the people I lived with and am living with are very strong. Over the years, I've learned to love and respect these people. I know them because I am one of them and part of them. If I don't write about them, nobody will.

The first man I felt I had to write about was Mike. I knew he was going to die, I knew he wanted to die. A few days after his funeral, I went to my old typewriter. I wanted to write about him badly: the kind of man he was, the things he told me about, and the world in which he existed, which had ended at least ten years earlier. Mike was my friend in a most unique way. And he had no other friends. As I sat behind my typewriter I realized I couldn't write about him. I still can't and that's several years later.

It was difficult for me to write about other people too: Dora and Freddy, the Irishman, Bill and the Polish family whose son stepped on a mine in Vietnam, my neighbor the gravedigger, and other people. And it's hard for me to write about myself. I am a private person, always have been. I don't believe in letting it all hang out. I've done things of which I am ashamed, of which I won't talk even to good friends. But I am also a part of this reality and as such I can't remain aloof. And so I write.

Once There Was a Village

Another winter, another house. Tonight, tomorrow, it's been some years.

I don't know, and why should I care? My quiet house on Seventh Street is only four blocks away. Might as well be four thousand miles.

The road to Eleventh Street led me first to the Upper West Side where I rented a tiny room in someone's huge apartment. In the dust of the singles bars and among burnt-out but very noisy film-makers, I don't quite remember what was happening. One night the mice ate all my Libriums; I went out, took the Broadway bus to the UN, walked all night, and in the morning found myself drinking Ripple with two old friends on Eleventh Street. Another friend stopped by. He introduced me to his super, a Ukrainian woman who had three rooms. I wanted more space, wanted to do some constructions. Maria, our beautiful super, was sitting there, drinking tea. Maria had a four-room apartment, and cheaper too, only sixty-four dollars. I paid more for my tiny room. I walked with her across the street and took it.

The apartment was in a very bad shape; the house, even worse. Junkies had a large shooting gallery in the basement. They were also shooting up on the stairs and on the roof. Every day I'd sweep dozens of waxed envelopes away from my door. And every other day, I'd find fresh sprays of blood on hallway walls and new knifemarks on the stairs where they sat playing with their toys.

A few days after I moved in, I put a lock on the front door and gave each tenant a key. Then I put a two-by-four across the door leading to the yard and a huge hook on the roof door. The junkies didn't like it—tough shit! Jim Richardson and his family moved in on the second floor. Together we reinforced our defenses and also told the junkies to take their shit out of our basement and not come back. At first they tried a few things, but soon they gave up on us and our house was relatively quiet from that time on.

Long four blocks from Seventh Street. What a difference.

Minutes jump by, and hours. My son slept badly last night. He couldn't get to sleep until about ten. When he finally fell asleep, the shooting began on my corner of Eleventh Street and Avenue B, and two cops lay dead in a big puddle of blood.

For a couple of seconds, I thought the shots were cherry bombs set off by some jerk. For a couple of seconds. It was a long time before the first squad car arrived. It was some night. My son was having bad dreams and I was watching a nightmare right from my window.

There's one place in the world where the concept of time loses all meaning—in the East Village, east of Avenue B. Years can go very fast, and days can drag on forever.

Tonight a huge moon came over the Con Ed chimneys; snow was melting along with garbage and dogshit. A large rat, completely freaked out, was running back and forth on the sidewalk in front of the Pioneer store on Avenue B. A junkie, equally freaked out, almost stepped on the rat. When he realized what it was, he jumped up, cursed, and ran back across Thirteenth Street to Dirty Stanley's. The rat circled in a daze until the fruitstand owner pushed her under the cars with a broom. I went into the liquor store and laid out a dollar for a bottle of Richard's Peach Wine. A fantastic combination I stumbled on once, by accident, Richard's Peach Wine and grass.

And it works even better when you have a woman you love next to you, and you touch her fingertips, and you're both suddenly in a bright world of waterfalls and children playing on the beach. And the sky feels like velvet when you're flying through it at an incredible speed. And those birch trees—touch those birches and it's like touching someone's soul. You enter into an even more mysterious world without space or dimension, where love is everywhere. Even while you're swimming through the octopus's insides, it's lovely, BEAUTIFUL! Richard's Peach Wine from Bonded Winery No. 21 in Virginia and plain old Mexican grass. Try it people, you'll like it.

Once There Was a Village

As I cross Thirteenth Street and B, I look east in amazement. The whole block, Thirteenth Street between Avenues B and C, is gone. Carpet-bombed, destroyed. And it used to be the worst block in all of Manhattan. I remember only a couple of months ago, Jimmy and I were scrounging through its empty, boarded-up tenements, picking up locks or a stove, or two-by-fours, or gates—whatever we could use in our house on Eleventh Street.

Rummaging through an abandoned building is a trip in itself. The buildings are dead, but they don't know it yet. There are still human spirits flying through the empty, fucked-up hallways, and every crumbling wall talks to you when you're willing to listen. And the layers of cheap linoleum are wondering whatever happened to all the tired feet that were scraping them day after day, night after night, for so many years—Irish feet, black and Puerto Rican feet, Ukrainian and hippie and, finally, the unsteady feet of the junkies. All gone.

And, wonder of wonders, a thing called Tanya Towers is being constructed in the middle of nowhere.

I cross the street and enter Dirty Stanley's. First time I've stopped there in years. Only one face looked familiar: Andy, the owner. The rest were hard junkie-ripoff faces measuring everyone who came in with their empty cash-register eyes. I KNEW at least three guys there KNEW, just by looking me over, I had exactly two dollars and fourteen cents in my pockets plus three more dollars in my sock. They also knew the bottle in my bag was Richard's (it's a square bottle).

One junkie playing pool bent down to get a better shot, and his knife, a folding red knife with a golden dragon on the handle, one of those Vietnamese knives which junkies love for some reason, fell out of his pocket. The guy was slightly embarrassed picking it up, and I got even more depressed.

An old man who didn't belong there was sitting in the corner by himself, drinking beer. I thought at first it was Mack. He looked like Mack—heavyset, worn-out brown overcoat, wide-rimmed hat. The only thing wrong was this man was black, and Mack was a Cossack colonel in the Great Cossack Army of the Don.

Mack came up through the ranks during the First World War and received the highest Russian decoration—the Order of St. George—for capturing a German artillery battery singlehanded.

During the Russian Civil War he fought with the Whites. Whenever his unit would capture a few Reds, he'd string them up, literally, by their balls. If he happened to catch a commissar, he'd order the man to drop his pants and bend down. Then Mack would personally shoot the man through the asshole with his large Mauser.

Nevertheless, the Reds managed to win the Civil War, and Mack fled to Yugoslavia. After other incredible adventures, including a few years as a supreme commander of the Albanian cavalry, he came to New York.

Mack came to America along with the thousands of other so-called displaced persons after the Second World War. (I was one of the DPs myself.) The first couple of years in America were rough on Mack. He was working as a dishwasher at the Blarney Stone on Sixth Avenue and hating every minute of his strenuous, nine-hour day. There was nothing else. And Mack couldn't speak English then. He finally collapsed from overwork and a heart attack and was hospitalized for three months.

This was the best thing that ever happened to him in America. In the hospital he met another Russian DP who was mopping floors in his ward, and that man introduced Mack to his foreman. They didn't have any openings at the hospital, but the foreman sent Mack to see another foreman and Mack landed a job mopping floors at night in Rockefeller Center. He loved that job. No one screamed at him any more, no one called him dumb-dumb. His crew was about equally divided between DPs of Russian and Ukrainian origin, and blacks. All were intelligent, friendly, and interesting men. The foreman, a gentle black man in his fifties who had two master's degrees and was just about finished with his doctorate, had only one worry: two Ukrainian newcomers were working too fast. Mack stayed with this job for over thirteen years, until he was forced to retire.

He was a fair chess-player when sober. When drunk, he was coming alive and was really very good. A rotten, rotten loser, though, drunk or sober. And anytime a woman would show up at the bar, he'd be sitting next to her within seconds, bending her ear with his heroic exploits and patting her thighs with his red, chubby hands. He was about eighty, I guess.

He had a wife who was a most cruel woman. We all knew she was hiding his money and starving him, and above all, she once flirted with a deacon of a small Russian church in New Jersey. That incident happened quite a few years back when they were visiting her relatives near the ROOVA farm, but it was always remarkably fresh in Mack's mind after his sixth or seventh beer.

"How could she do it?" he was wondering aloud, opening wide his small piggish eyes and banging on the table with his beer mug. He couldn't understand what his wife saw in the tiny, puny-looking deacon who, it was rumored, was a queer besides.

After his ninth or tenth beer, he was no longer upset, because the truth by now was all too apparent. His wife was simply in a conspiracy with her sister to drive him insane (with jealousy) and lock him up in some old folks' home. Something which he dreaded.

Mack could usually be found at Old Stanley's (now usually called Dirty Stanley's) around the first and fifteenth of each month. That's when his checks came in and his wife, mean as she was, would give him a few bucks to buy the first few beers. The rest of the beer and vodka was bought by his friends. And, surprisingly enough, Mack had many friends. I was his friend, too, although at times I couldn't stand the sight of him. Mack liked me because aside from playing chess, lending him a couple of bucks, or buying him a few drinks when I was working, I was one of two people he could speak Russian with. The other guy was Dimitri, the young Ukrainian poet, who was then still working for the Department of Welfare. Mack liked Dimka less—Dimka was tighter with his money and he didn't play chess. Mack's Russian was excellent. In fact, in his spare time he wrote very long and very detailed letters to New York's Russian newspapers, *Novoye Russkoye Slovo* and *Rossiya*. His letters were always regarding the Russian Civil War, and they took apart all other writers on that subject. He sometimes showed me his letters and they were good. Probably not at all accurate, harsh and sarcastic and totally reactionary, but they were lively.

One night I had to take Mack home. He was throwing up all over the place, falling down on the sidewalk, and kicking garbage cans.

"Leave me alone, let me die," he kept screaming. "Let me die like a dog." In the hallway of his house he sobered up a little. He leaned on the stairs and looked straight at me, but I don't think he even saw me or the yellowed wall full of cockroaches. He might have been looking over his River Don—a wide silver snake in the endless steppes. Over the white houses of a Cossack village and the poplar trees. And maybe he was hearing sounds of an accordion in the clear evening air or saw a young Cossack jumping on his horse and galloping along the river bank toward the next village to meet his woman.

Tears were streaming down Mack's fat cheeks. He said, "I'll die like a dog and I'll go down to hell, I know it."

He crossed himself. "You live like a dog, and like a dog you will die . . ." With that pronouncement, he started up the stairs.

He somehow made it, found his keys and opened his door. For a second I saw his wife. She was a very small woman. She looked tired and worried, a typical Russian grandmother with a kind, wrinkled face.

She helped him in and carefully shut the door.

Through the door I heard Mack screaming at her, sounds of sobbing and something heavy falling on the floor.

Later on that night, I had all kinds of nightmares. And soon afterward, my own life disintegrated to the point of real nightmare and I wound up on the seventh floor of good old Bernstein Institute. After I got out, I went back to Old Stanley's a few times, but I never ran into Mack.

The whole scene was changing anyway. Many of my friends were leaving the East Village; others were digging deeper into their own trenches, preparing for a hard winter. Bill Schneider's red hair and beard were not seen at Stanley's any more. Gone were the days when he was presiding over our group, buying drinks and entertaining us with his stories. Bill sold his great pornographic novel, bought a motorcycle, and took off in the direction of his hometown, somewhere in the state of Washington. Ann went to Texas, then to New Hampshire or Maine. Dimitri also freaked out and found himself on welfare. Another good friend hit acid as if it were going out of style. Some friends began shooting speed and shit. And it became too dangerous to get drunk at Old Stanley's: Nearly everybody was ripped off on the way home. And, after a neighbor of mine had his throat sliced and died later on in Bellevue, I stopped going to Old Stanley's myself.

Now, a couple of years later (or was it only a few days?), I am sitting where Mack used to sit, by the same broken window, and I am thinking of him. God rest his soul, even if he's still alive.

I see the famous orange cat walking under my table. That cat is something else again, and then some. He'll live forever. On one of the afternoons, one of those long summers, I was drinking beer with Emilio and that cat dragged in a half-dead mouse. He played with the mouse on the floor, jumped up on one of the empty tables, and proceeded to eat it while the mouse was still squeaking and squirming. We were getting ready to barf when one of the women at the bar stood up, pulled the mouse out of the cat's jaws, and threw it out of the window on Avenue B. This same window.

The old man whom I almost mistook for Mack is leaving, followed by two ripoffs. I finish my beer and go home, holding on to my Richard's.

On my corner on Eleventh Street, there are still two TV cameras and lights, and some bystanders with their dogs. But the puddles of policemen's blood are now much smaller.

I certainly hope I am dreaming. My glass is heavy now because it's empty.

My loft bed decided to walk around the room.

I look very closely into my round red construction. It's another planet with cities and valleys, and I'd like very much to take off my skin and my body and crawl under one of the smaller piano-pieces to find out what's happening on the other side.

I don't exist anyway.

I only lived when mornings were fresh and the forget-me-nots were growing in our lovely garden. I was running with my textbooks, always late, down the wide Stalin Boulevard to my school—Railroad School No. 2. And our old dog was following me to the end of the chestnut trees and would come back to meet me there after classes. I'd play with her, make her chase me, and give her a part of my sandwich.

Stop walking, you stupid bed. Go to sleep and let me sleep.

Useless. So fucking useless.

Maybe the junkies are on to something—die as fast as you can and avoid all the bullshit. Maybe everybody's right. Acidheads and speed freaks, and health-food people, and Yoga and karate freaks, and the kids who jerk off on their knives.

And maybe the old Richard's formula is not working so well tonight.

Our backyard, our beautiful backyard, the eleventh wonder of Eleventh Street.

An inspiration to me on my gloomy days, a source of joy and amazement. I open the heavy piece of plywood blocking my window and sunshine pours into my kitchen. I get out on the fire escape with a cup of coffee and I look down at about two dozen cats in our yard, all colors, all shapes.

Watching the cats gets rid of even my Russian melancholy. Some of these cats sit in incredible poses on our fence, which in itself is quite incredible. It's made from old doors, pieces of plywood, wire bedsprings, and boards of all shapes and colors, and it's propped up by some beams and held together by wire, rope, God knows what. It doesn't really serve any purpose—any kid can climb over it—but it does provide a great place for a cat to catch some sun.

On one of the boards, the best board, sprawls my favorite: an old white cat, a gorgeous creature. He doesn't care about anything except the morning sun, and he's going to catch every last ounce of it. His ears are completely gone, long ago bitten off by fleas, ticks, and other cats. He must be more than ten years old. He has seen all there is to see, and he knows all there is to know. His head is misshapen from countless bruises and scratches, and the rest of his body is no better. I believe he can only see with one eye. He's stretching and I'm stretching.

Under him, in the yard, the grass is knee-deep. There are many plants and flowers which Maria, our super, planted two years ago. That's her private Ukrainian garden right there. She keeps it clean, she feeds the cats, and she tries to keep everyone else out of there. The cats slink through the grass and bushes as though they were tigers in a deep jungle. My dog and Jimmy's dog, who are sometimes permitted in the yard, don't bother the cats at all. And the cats don't bother the dogs. Everyone gets along.

Observing the cats in action, one has to realize that we humans, supposedly the smartest of species, are plain stupid when it comes to life, love, coexistence, and death.

The white cat will not move until the last ray of sun leaves the stump that once was his tail, around eleven o'clock. Then he'll go to sleep behind the boiler or maybe chase some young kitty. He's in semiretirement. If only he could write his memoirs.

On Eleventh Street, between Avenues B and C (our block is known as "little Nam" although I've been told by a few friends who returned from Vietnam that they felt much safer over there), the summer comes early and stays forever.

At least so it seems when I'm trying to sleep around three in the morning and a couple of addicts are screaming outside my window. Dogs are barking, cats and sirens are howling, and some guy is playing the same record over and over again, full blast. And there's no more beer in my icebox.

I close my eyes in resignation and immediately hear two squadrons of mosquitoes divebombing at my tired head and body. I jump up, wipe the cold sweat from my forehead, and start examining the cracks in the walls, the pipes, and the ceiling. Nothing. Just a few flies circling by the lightbulb. Not a single mosquito anywhere. Maybe I was sleeping? Maybe it was all a bad dream? Sure, that's what it was. I turn off the light. And when I wake up with quite a few welts upon my head and my body, I usually look in the mirror and ponder the complexity of nature. The most painful paradox of it being that the mosquitoes have more brains and guts than I do. And then, they bite.

People are always telling me, "Buy the Shell strip, Baby, buy this Six-Twelve spray." Bullshit. Last summer I hung three Shell strips in my apartment, one right over my bed, and the mosquitoes still ate me up. The sprays help for an hour, two at the outside. The repellents don't work at all. Our mosquitoes are virtually indestructible. They are an ultrasophisticated city-slum breed—they'll live through anything. If you'd been born in some flooded basement, you'd be indestructible too.

Our basements are always flooded during the summer. And what a great place they are for observing our insects and other wildlife.

Once There Was a Village

When I was repairing a boiler a few weeks ago, I saw a touching scene: Mother rat was swimming across the black lake followed by four or five cute baby rats, just like a duck followed by a string of ducklings. I saw a flotilla of water beetles, about fifteen of them, hooked together in the water, next to a wall, helping one another make it up the slithery pipe into a large crack in the wall. To get to the boiler, I had to brush my way past several families of spiders—most of them were dark brown and mean-looking, but one family was pale blue and somehow not too menacing.

I had to be careful not to step on a colony of centipedes —they were each about an inch long and an inch wide and were pink with black spots. There were other insects in that basement that almost defy description. One guy looked like a black worm about three inches long, but he had a green fluorescent head with large eyes and coming from behind his head were two claws, like a small scale lobster. And he was fast. I saw him, he saw me, he dived under some catshit and was gone, in less than a second. Goodbye!

I have a sculptor friend, Jeff, who swore to me he had things which looked like large scorpions living in his store-front on Ninth Street. He had it so bad that he was more afraid of them than of muggers. Recently his cat died under mysterious circumstances. Bitten by one of those things. And Jeff moved out somewhere toward Second Avenue.

I didn't see any scorpions, but I did see a fantastic thing, direct from the Sahara Desert, which Jimmy Richardson caught in his bedroom. This is well-documented —everyone in our house saw it and was impressed. It looked like a long spider, about four inches in length with a small head and thin legs, about twenty of them, each about two inches long with claws on the end, and furry. In fact, the whole thing was furry. Its color was orange. Jimmy kept it in a jar and fed it flies for a while, but the thing withered and died. I'd really like to know what it was.

A while ago, on a bright warm morning, Jimmy and I were repairing the trapdoor leading from our yard into our basement. Most of the doorframe was rotten and had to be replaced; we had to pour cement to steady the part of it with the hinges. When we tore away the old four-by-fours, underneath, in the soft black earth, was a small world all by itself—the world of black spiders and centipedes, ants, worms, cockroaches, green beetles, all kinds of beetles, and a rainbow of other bugs—all scurrying around, hopping mad that their life had been disrupted and that they'd been evicted. Watching them, we somehow felt better. The bulldozers tearing up Twelfth Street seemed far, far away. The Con Ed smokestacks with their black clouds, even farther. And the fact that we didn't have enough money to get us a couple of cans of beer didn't bother us any more.

The summer of 1972 it happened, the inevitable. People began looking like bugs to me. For example, I leaned out of my front window and I saw a group of addicts congregating on the corner of Eleventh and B. Two of them were definitely fleas, hopping up and down and around. One guy looked and acted like a big tick; he was the dealer. And the fourth one was a cockroach running from one corner to another, trying to hustle something. Two cops walked on the other side of B. They were heavy: waterbeetles. A hippie chick hurried by, tall and very thin—she was a mosquito. I don't want to continue further because this harmless delusion might grow and get me locked up again in some mental ward.

There's one person, however, whom I can't get out of my mind, who so much resembles a pale, fragile spring butterfly. Hopelessly lost in the heat of summer.

When I was a boy in the North Caucasus, the appearance of the first butterfly was a special event. And the earlier the first butterflies were sighted, the better the year was going to be. If very large numbers of early spring butterflies were sighted, everyone knew it was going to be another "butterfly summer," when everything would grow in overabundance and the weather would be unusually good.

The summer of 1942 was the butterfly summer.

But it was not a good summer.

It brought about the breakup of our family and the beginning of a never-ending odyssey for me, a hassle of growing up, somehow surviving through the war and after the war, and still trying to survive in a very strange country that became my homeland. A homeland which I love and hate at the same time, just like Russia.

The German army made a breakthrough at Rostov and moved very fast through the North Caucasian steppes, wheat fields, and Cossack villages.

In the morning our radio told us: "The fighting rages near Salsk [a town about one hundred kilometers north of us]. All German attacks were valiantly beaten back."

Around noon we were bombed, very heavily bombed.

In the afternoon, we saw Russian soldiers running across our yards and through the gardens. Some of them were throwing away their rifles and changing as fast as they could into civilian clothing. We heard some cannon fire and bursts of machinegun fire.

In the evening, the food stores were looted. There were no more militia men in sight. Later in the evening, the first German units came through the city.

A few weeks earlier, my mother had been arrested on some idiotic charge of saying something against Stalin. We knew it was one of our neighbors who turned her in. He wanted a part of our tiny one-and-a-half-room apartment. My father couldn't do very much. Only two years before, he himself had returned from a concentration camp, one of the few survivors of the Great Purge of 1937. He even lived and worked in the city illegally. Still, he went to the NKVD and demanded to see the prosecutor. The prosecutor was unusually polite. He said my mother was merely being held on suspicion and, once we had been evacuated, everything would be fine. Everyone would be happily reunited.

We were packed and waiting for the truck when the bombs started to fall.

There was, of course, no truck.

Usually we had lots of air alarms, sirens, and loudspeakers, and no planes. This time the alarm was given only after most of the bombs were already dropped.

We had a garden, tended first by my grandmother when she was alive, then by my mother, then by me. I was in our garden when the bombing began. I was supposed to hide across the street in our new school. I started running there, but the school was already in ruins and all the people in its basement were killed.

I returned and sat in our garden. Several small incendiary bombs fell into our yard, one into our garden, a few steps from me, and one fell into our attic. I had to climb up and push it out of there—it had only partially exploded—and pour water on the beams that were on fire.

In the midst of all that smoke and explosions—this I'll never forget—swarms of butterflies were flying aimlessly and falling on the ground overwhelmed by the smoke and shock. By the fence of our garden, some lilac bushes grew wild. The ground beneath these bushes was covered with bodies of yellow and white butterflies.

I noticed them only because I was a boy; grownups don't look at these things. Not in the middle of bombing.

I haven't seen any real butterflies so far this year, not even in our beautiful backyard.

But what's a reality?

Thirty-four abandoned cars were burned on our block this summer. I counted them myself. And many of these cars were burned two or three times. People killed and mugged, a dear friend committing suicide, another friend freaking out. The poverty, the garbage, the pollution.

Is that the reality?

I prefer to think of my pale spring butterfly.

I can't help but think of her anyway.

On my long sleepless nights I write love poems to her in my mind. Wherever she happens to be, I feel I can always touch her.

I play Yulia's records, over and over, until I am almost crying.

I look at her cheerful postcards and I transplant myself into some clean European city and walk beside her, and sit beside her in a sidewalk cafe.

I want to tell her how much I love her and how everything else is meaningless, and what a stupid, fucked-up idiot I've been. And how profoundly sorry I am. I sit there, but I can't say it. Too late. Far too late.

I walk through museums and castles, cathedrals and parks.

I look at my son, sleeping quietly, breathing evenly.

I am wondering whether she'll ever come back.

I am on a train to Copenhagen, in a bar of a Danish fishing village. I have to tell her how much I need her, every inch of her, so familiar to my skin. Her yellow hair.

It's misty while the ferry takes us to Harwich. Lonely sounds of ship horns passing one another in the North Sea. We are sitting on deck, close to one another.

I am holding her hand. I am holding her hand.

I need her smile, her sunny, funny disposition, her warmth.

I need to hear her say, "I love you, baby, God, I love you so much," as she said several lifetimes ago. I am drinking red wine and I'll take three Libriums instead of the usual two. I'll work on my constructions until my eyes will close. Until I won't be able to open them again.

I have to get up early tomorrow and take my son to school. I have to set the alarm clock. I have to see the man who is interested in buying one of my smaller piano constructions. I have to go downtown to check on my current show.

I have to do this and that. I have to, I have to, I have to.

Stop it! I don't have to. Not yet. Not just yet.

I am on a train to Lisbon. I am walking on a beach. Most tourists are gone, and the fishermen are out at sea. Portugal is lovely in late September.

She's lovely any time of the year. I don't even have a good portrait of her. I don't need it. I know every line on her face. I could paint her portrait now.

She's so fragile and sensitive, and I understand.

I can't express myself, but I understand.

Her wings are tired and bruised, the summer is nearly over.

Too many years ran their heavy time into an ocean.

All is gray now and we're drowning in it.

Too many mistakes, they don't matter any more.

In beautiful Lisbon, another man perhaps will pour her a glass of wine.

I refuse to give up.

I think of the old white cat, licking his new wounds on our roof. All night long he's been fighting, even through my stupor I've heard his screams.

If I only knew how to fight right now. When all feelings are in the past and, whether I like it or not, I have to cope with the reality which is here, today and tomorrow.

The reality is like quicksand: The more you get into it, the quicker you'll sink. At least I have my art—the rope lowered to me from heaven to help me over the big swamp. I lose that rope and I'll be sunk for sure.

I wish I had to fight a clearcut issue. Like that cat, like I did in postwar Germany. Simply a question of survival.

When I was thirteen, we had a good Russian gang over there, four of us. We called ourselves "Russian Falcons." We were the only foreign kids in a large German village, population one thousand. We all went to the Russian gymnasium in Stuttgart, about thirty kilometers by train. We usually came home at night and had to go through the whole village, enemy territory, to our house on the outskirts. And every night, German boys were waiting for us in ambush. The Germans would not just jump you and beat you up; it's not in their character. They'd surround you first and thoroughly insult you, making sure that your ego was beaten into the ground. Then they'd beat you up.

Late one night. A few houses on one side of the street, a field on the other, a perfect place for an ambush. I am walking home by myself. I told my Russian friends to go home around the village. I know the Germans are about to strike. I come to one of the fences. I pull out a twig from a hiding place. Not an ordinary twig—this one is a radio antenna I sawed off an American tank, a piece of nice springy steel. I also take out my bayonet from my boot and place it atop my rucksack on my back, in which I carry my books, so that I can take it out instantly. A few hundred meters later, a small bridge, another perfect spot. I am exactly in the middle of the bridge when they appear. Three ahead of me and three in back of me. They start hurling the usual racial insults and showing me their clubs and knives. I wait, my back to the railing. I hold my antenna behind me so they don't see it.

Germans hate the unexpected. They are happy that I am alone, they don't have to fight so much. Also, they think I am the leader. But they are a little wary; why didn't I try to run away? They think I am probably petrified, that's why. They are partly right. I am afraid. But I am more angry than afraid.

As soon as they come into a semicircle around me, I start swinging my antenna, catching them in their faces. Again and again, on their faces, on their hands, on their legs, as fast as I can. I didn't think they'd run, but run they did, all six of them, screaming and cursing and vowing revenge. A couple even dropped their clubs.

There was no revenge. Our gang soon thereafter went into the wallet-making business. We found, in the French zone, a warehouse full of choicest leather, and we also found a Russian bootmaker. We put two and two together and had ourselves a very profitable racket. We were selling our wallets in Stuttgart to American soldiers, and we sold them in the Armenian refugee camp, in the Jewish refugee camp and in the Ukrainian refugee camp, all around Stuttgart. We quickly became rich by German standards, corrupted, and school dropouts.

Nobody bothered us any more. We had all the weapons we needed. The German kids stopped attacking us and German cops stopped their harassment. We were growing up very fast.

We stopped masturbating together on the banks of the not-so-beautiful Neckar River and we threw away our tin can. That tin can was helping to provide amusement. We used to place it by a weeping willow and stand away from it a few steps and masturbate with the idea of spraying into the can. Sounds silly now; then it was fun. We gave it all up to take up women.

I vaguely remember my early involvements. There was a pretty German girl from our village, another in Stuttgart, an Armenian girl, a Polish girl; there were prostitutes and married women and widows. The world at that time was so different, so unique. After the horrors of war, everyone wanted so much to catch up on living, and sex was rediscovered as being so much a part of living. The only thing that kept a rein on me was the fear of catching VD, which all three other members of the "Russian Falcons" had caught and which delayed their departures to Canada, Venezuela, and Australia, respectively.

What was wrong with all that? I grew up too fast and too far in some areas, and in some I didn't grow up at all.

One one hand I had this Russian morality hanging over me, which is much more Victorian than Victorian morality; on the other was the enticement of sin (sex)—totally physical, readily available, and always enjoyable.

Only years later did I discover a simple elusive ingredient called love—an element that breaks down the ideologies and upbringings and elevates a person from a state of being into a state of being alive.

I was alive for a while. Now I am back in the state of being and I resent it.

And I refuse to give up.

A dream shakes me up almost every morning. Our

Christmas tree is tall and beautiful. The decorations she has saved over the years are reflected in a warm, golden glow. It's very late at night. I am very tired. I stand by the Christmas tree alone and I look at my son's presents, and a frightening thought enters my mind—she's not in the apartment. I am petrified. I can't breathe. Then the alarm clock rings softly in her bedroom. I open the door. She sits on the bed in her lovely red nightgown. She smiles; her large green eyes are friendly, twinkling. She smiles—that's the best sight for me, dream or reality. She says, "Come here, baby." I wake up, it's almost five in the morning. I can still feel her skin.

I swallow some cold water, wipe my sweat. I know my rooster will soon crow downstairs in an empty storefront. He does, at five fifteen, as usual. He is a happy, healthy rooster. He was raised for cockfights, but the building where he was kept burned down. He somehow escaped to the roof and fell into a shaft of a tenement across from mine. Two Ukrainian women pulled him out of there, and one night he was given to me. I kept him in my apartment for two weeks. Which was quite an experience. Maria, our great super, took him off my hands and installed him in the store downstairs. She still takes care of him and he's quite contented. He crows again and I feel less shaky. I slowly pull myself together.

The morning sun breaks through the Con Ed chimneys as I take my dog into our yard.

My head aches. I am disgusted with myself for sliding into the morass of self-pity, of not being able to control it.

I watch the cats. The white one is on his board on the fence, as usual. My dog is running around, sniffing things out. From one of Maria's rosebushes (I've got to be dreaming!) flies out a tiny white butterfly and then two more, slightly larger. My dumb dog runs after them, tries to catch them.

I jump up and yell, "Igor, stop!"

She stops and looks at me as though to say, "What's the

matter, master, you've flipped? It's only a butterfly."

ONLY A BUTTERFLY? The three butterflies are safe on a taller bush. I can't believe it. I walk up to take a closer look. They're there.

They are REAL. I could even catch them if I wanted to.

It's such a great omen, and right now I am ready to clutch at any good omen. I think perhaps with me it's the other way around, as usual, instead of early butterflies, late butterflies.

Maybe my summer is not yet over, maybe it's about to begin. Butterfly summer.

I am walking with her from our San Francisco apartment all the way to Sausalito and back. We stop on the Golden Gate Bridge and look at the boats, at the city. We buy some souvenir in Sausalito; we stop to see my show there, in a tiny gallery. I only painted seascapes at that time. Oils, watercolors, pen-and-inks, some good, some not so good. We come back and fall into our bed exhausted.

I wonder what she's thinking about in Paris.

I remember when we were painting the ceiling of our coffeehouse. The ceiling was so high I was afraid to stand on top of the ladder, but she climbed up and did it, no sweat. And the Red and Herb bar and, again, our apartment, our friends now scattered as far as Copenhagen on one side and Australia on the other.

Where is that famous photograph where we are standing behind our gleaming double-unit Faema expresso machine?

I must go! I call my dog. I can't see the butterflies any more, but I know they are there. And all the other bugs and animals and people. And everyone is busy trying to hustle, to survive, each in his own way. Even butterflies. Even spring butterflies.

I hope so much she'll survive. I hope her wings will heal and she'll soar high in the blue. And we shall meet again in a friendly meadow under the warm sun.

Miracles do happen. This I believe. I've lived through a few.

I need one more.

I need my spring butterfly very badly.

I must lift myself up and get going.

So much to do. I promised my son I'd meet him at the Tompkins Square Park at noon and take him to the Odessa for lunch. Their school lunches are terrible. I can't be late. I have other things to do. I have to, I have to.

There are men who'll do anything for a woman and she will not be interested.

Jack was the kind of guy who would take one look at a woman and she'd melt. And should he look at a woman twice, the woman knew she would be laid by this gorgeous half-man, half-child, half-animal. Tonight, tomorrow, Where? Anywhere. Nothing mattered except his very slanted dark eyes, wide cheekbones, full mouth closed in a dreamy half-smile, and long flaming red hair resting on his slender shoulders.

Summer, Saturday, and as usual, I am sitting in Tompkins Square Park playing chess with one of the old men. Jeff, my sculptor friend, stops by with Jack and introduces us. Jack wants to play the winner; I happened to win. We play a game. It's a good tough game. I know I am winning, yet the game goes back and forth; I am ahead and when I look again, he's ahead. I know I am playing this young kid and I should've won twenty moves ago. I am supposed to be one of the best players around here. And around here, everybody plays good chess. Finally, I sacrifice my bishop, open up his king with my queen and my knight, block his queen with my other knight. Nothing he can do; it's a mate situation. And checkmate it is! That's it! I look at Jack, and I look again—at the face of a furious old man. Every wrinkle stands out, every vein on his slightly freckled face, lower lip hanging down defensively; his teeth are coming out as if he's going to jump over the table and bite me. Undisguised hatred in his Chinese eyes.

"You were lucky," Jack says.

"Sure," I agree. Whenever I win a game, I always say to my opponent, "I was lucky." And I still don't know whether it's the humility in me or an ego trip. Maybe a bit of both.

"Let's bet five on the next game," Jack says, his face back to normal. Jeff quietly laughs beside me. "Jack hates losing. He's a Russian prick too."

"You're Russian?" I ask him in Russian.

"So what?" he answers in Russian with a heavy accent. "Give Jeffrey your five and here's mine."

He pulls out a fat roll of bills, gives five to Jeff. It's up to me.

It's a kind of trap situation where your ego and your manhood are already on the line. Fortunately, I have five bucks today.

I have this ritual to go through first, however. It's in the nature of psychological warfare.

I say, "Look, you're sure you want to do it? When I play for money, I don't lose, not ever." Which is true, by the way, but it always helps to get their nerves jumping.

"That's O.K.," Jack says, "Neither do I."

A few moves and I make a terrible blunder, a beginner's error and he's a castle ahead. And his position is better than mine. This is getting very bad.

I concentrate on the only chance I've got, and that's getting through to his king. It's a wild game. I am sacrificing a knight in the process and two of my pawns. Materially speaking, he's won the game. But now I have a good attack going which he can't stop because his figures are all over the board. I am sitting right on top of his king, protected only by his queen which is lost—an exchange of his queen for my castle! From here on, it's pure slaughter. He's avoided a mate but my queen is at his king's throat. Free to check and take his unprotected pieces. Which is exactly what I do —check him, take his castle, take his knight, his other castle.

He's through, he knows it, but he plays to the end, desperately trying to push his pawns through. Which is pathetic. I take them one by one. Then a checkmate.

Again the wrinkled face of an old wolf ready to jump me.

It's Tompkins Square Park, Saturday afternoon. Friendly vibrations all over, for a change. Kids playing their drums, hippies walking their dogs, old men playing cards and checkers, a pair of lovers sitting on the grass in an embrace, smoking pot; old women sitting on their benches soaking in the sun, even two cops standing by the men's room. Love and peace are in the air.

And here I am sitting, my hand in my back pocket where my knife is, because I have this strange feeling about Jack, and I am a great believer in feelings.

Jeff the sculptor is worried too. He's smiling, but I can see he's worried.

"You should've lost!" Jack tells me in Russian. Jeff understands some Russian. He stops smiling.

"I was lucky," I tell him in Russian. "I said I never lose for money."

Jack flips. He jumps up and yells at me every possible obscenity for a minute or two, in English (I guess he didn't know how to swear in Russian too well). All heads are turning our way, even the cops. Jack stops abruptly, tells Jeff, "Let's go," and starts walking. Jeff hands me the money. Jeff says, "Yuri, don't worry. Jack's a nice guy. He really is." He hurries to catch up with Jack.

I sit for a moment and contemplate the empty chessboard and try to get myself together. Jeffrey and Jack are walking toward Avenue A. Jack is even walking strangely—with each step his whole body moves, like a cat.

It occurs to me now why I held my hand on my knife. Jack is a dope fiend from the word DOPE. I don't know how I failed to notice it right away. He is heavily into it. I wondered how he pays for his shit. It's now quite expensive.

Not in ripoffs, not with his good mind. Dealing? Maybe, except he didn't behave like a dealer. The dealer never worries about heroin, he's got all he could use. That's why the dealer is always cool. Jack wasn't cool at all. Yet he had at least a couple of hundred in his roll. I wondered what his thing was.

The answer came sooner than I expected.

A friend of mine, a beautiful blonde from Wisconsin, Helen, seventeen, had disappeared.

I was somewhat involved with her sexually, but mostly it was just good friendship and kidding around. She was staying with another chick on Tenth Street near Second Avenue and worked nights as a cocktail waitress. She was young but very hip and certainly knew all there was to know about sex. At least as far as I know sex. I was trying to find her an apartment in exchange for which she promised me more of her orifices and other good things. I found an apartment, but I couldn't find Helen. She was last seen by anybody walking with Jack on Sixth Street toward Avenue D.

Another guy came looking for her, and the girl with whom Helen was staying became worried. It wasn't like Helen not to leave word.

A day or two later I bumped into Jack.

"Seen Helen?" I asked.

He was startled, like he'd just seen a ghost. He said, "No."

I said, "Like maybe a couple of days ago?"

"I haven't seen her in weeks. She probably went home," he lied.

I knew Helen couldn't go back home. I only couldn't understand why he was lying.

That's all right, I thought, I'll find out. There's very little that goes on in the East Village that one of my friends won't know about. I went to work. I talked to a few people who knew Jack, including Jeff the sculptor; talked to some of my customers in the bar who knew EVERYTHING. The more I heard, the more depressed and angry I became. And when I was coming home that night, there was Jack and another guy whom I didn't know waiting for me in my hallway. And they both had their knives open. Which was their mistake.

It gave me time to pull out mine and roll my shoulderbag around my left hand to use as a shield. I was in a good position. Our hallway is very narrow, just enough room for one person. So the second guy is really useless unless he's in back of you. The second guy, seeing my knife out (my knife is a little bigger than the ones they are holding), says something like, "Excuse me, sir," and splits.

It's between Jack and me. I keep swinging after Jack and try to get him off balance with my left hand. I am also forcing him into the corner by my door so he can't run off. All the time, he's snarling at me with his teeth and making faces, trying to distract me from watching his eyes. He is definitely not as good in a knife fight as he is at playing chess. Anyway, I cut over his arm. He sees the blood coming through his shirt and he loses some of his composure. He says something like, "Stop it, man, you're crazy. Let's talk. We'll both get killed."

I tell him to drop his knife. He drops it. He has no choice. I pick it up carefully. I say, "What do you want to talk about?"

"You've been asking everybody. Get off my back."

"Why you so uptight?"

"Listen, I'll kill you. I am not kidding. Get off my back!"

"Where's Helen?" I ask him.

"I don't know."

That does it for me. I jump up to him and in the good mugger tradition put my knife across his throat. I press it so he's forced to lift his head and look straight into the ceiling. I tell him I have every right to kill him and kill him I will if he doesn't start talking. He seems doubtful that I will, thinking maybe that artists don't quite behave like I do. That I am just scaring him. I cut him slightly to draw blood.

He talks. "Helen's working in the Bronx, in a social club. She's O.K."

By now I know what he means.

I tell him, "Get her back."

"I can't."

"Buy her back or you're through. How much was it anyway?"

Jack is angry and now he's frightened too. He can't move. He's caught like a rat. My knife is stuck to his throat. A little bit of blood is running down my blade and between my fingers. I am worried. What if somebody comes into the building? I believe if he hadn't started talking I'd have cut him from ear to ear without the slightest hesitation.

"I got two bills for her [two hundred dollars] but I CAN'T GET HER BACK!"

"You get her back tomorrow." I fold my knife, put it in my fist, and hit him as hard as I can in his balls.

I step over him, and go to my apartment. I know he'll bring her back.

He's a very smart guy; he'll find a way. He knows me now and he knows some of my friends. He realizes full well what will happen to him if Helen's not back.

The next day she's back, what's left of her.

What I didn't know at the time, the motherfucking son of a bitch had traded her back for two new runaways who were never heard from again. Ever.

Jack drops out of sight for a while.

A couple of months later, I stop by to visit Helen at the NYU hospital's psychiatric ward. Helen is thin, thoughtful, quiet, not full of life and laughter as she once was. She looks now like a forty-year-old woman. She's not yet eighteen. She will be getting out in another month or so. She wants to move out of the city. She knows a commune in Vermont she'd like to live in.

She talks very matter of factly about what happened to her after she'd gone to stay with Jack.

She went to him because she thought he was the handsomest guy she'd ever seen, and she wanted to fuck with him. Which is what they did the first night. He wasn't so great in bed, but it was nice enough. She was falling in love with him. The second day Jack slipped her some sunshine.

Once There Was a Village

Helen had dropped acid before but nothing as strong as that. Then a guy whom she didn't know came in and started fucking her. She told Jack that it was him she loved, she didn't want somebody else. Jack said it was a good friend; just do him a favor. The guy finished and left and another guy came in. She was freaking out at the time and didn't much care until the guy put on a French tickler (which she never had before) and used it both back and front and also began beating her with his belt. As freaked-out as she was, she started screaming. The guy stopped abruptly and left.

Later that night, Jack gave her something that knocked her out. She remembered very vaguely riding in a car with him and another guy. She woke up on a mattress in an empty storefront. One of her legs was held by a pair of police handcuffs attached to a motorcycle chain that was wrapped around a pipe and had a lock on it. She could only walk around a little. Through the cracks in the boarded-up windows, she could see a part of the street. Looked exactly like the East Village. There was a Latin club across the street. Children were playing; a fire hydrant was open. A man came in and brought her beans and rice with a pork chop and a can of beer. He told her not to worry. He also told her never to scream or she would be very badly punished. She stayed at the storefront four days and nights. People were reasonably decent to her; most of them were Dominicans. They simply fucked her, one at a time, and not more than seven in one night.

The storefront was a distribution point. While staying in the storefront, she saw three other girls come and go and she even spoke with them.

The other girls did not come from Jack, but they were all runaways.

One was twelve and she was crying most of the time.

From the storefront, Helen was resold to a sadist who kept her in a completely dark room on a short chain. He did not give her enough food and beat her for hours at a time. She was allowed to scream, but her room, in addition to being black, was also soundproof. When Helen was alone, she couldn't hear anything. Her "owner" threatened to torture her and kill her, and she believed him. He was also feeding her acid or perhaps a combination of acid and speed. She was losing her mind. He never fucked her or asked her to do anything. That, too, was frightening but just as frightening was the fact that she was losing her mind. She didn't know what time it was, whether it was day or night or anything. She knew he was going to kill her sooner or later. She was praying it would be soon.

That's when Jack arrived. Her knight in shining armor, she thought. Her "owner" unchained her, put a blindfold over her eyes. They went past some garbage cans into a car. She was allowed to take off the blindfold only when she entered her house on Tenth Street just before the door of her girlfriend's apartment.

Her girlfriend called me (I had my old Studebaker then), and we took Helen to the hospital.

Needless to say, I cannot speak about some of the things she told me because they are so sad and because they still concern her new family.

Jack surfaced, as sure as hell is hot.

It's a nice clear autumn day, the leaves in Tompkins Square Park are almost all yellow. Soon it will be noontime recess, and children from all the schools around will come running and playing through the park, living it up for forty-five minutes. I walk across the park to my bus stop and I see Jack standing on the corner of Tenth Street and A, looking his usual beautiful self. He's talking to two young hippie chicks. He's back in business. I pass him.

He throws me a quick, "We have no quarrel now, right, brother?" in Russian.

And in Russian I answer, "Lose yourself, you piece of dogshit."

He yells after me, "Yuri, I'm clean!" I am surprised he remembers my name. I stop and go back to him.

One of the chicks with him is a nice, happy-looking blonde. Wisconsin? Pennsylvania? Ohio? New Jersey? She's small-boned, delicate. My younger daughter is taller than she is.

She asks me, "Man, why do you shave your head?"

"I look better that way."

She laughs. It's a clean, infectious laugh.

Jack now hangs onto a heavy cane. I guess he's lost faith in knives.

He looks at me with a sly expression, as though to say, "Look, man, you want to fuck any of these two chicks, just say the word. They're yours. Be my guest. I am clean. I got nothing to hide."

He may be clean, but there's a worried look too in his Chinese eyes.

He doesn't know what I am going to do and it bothers him.

I tell him in Russian, "Relax, brother. Stay in good health. Get out of this city. Otherwise, one day soon, somebody will kill you."

"But I am not dealing anymore, I swear it."

He lies. I know it and he knows I know it.

He recently sold a brother and a sister, one twelve, the other thirteen. They were kept in a cellar on Eleventh Street only a block from where I live. They were fed dog-food because their "owner" was on some far-out kick and kept them with his three German shepherds. Fortunately, I don't know what he did with them and the shepherds and I don't want to know. I very nearly lost my life trying to free them. Unsuccessfully. For the first time, I phoned an anonymous tip to the cops. The cops were late getting there. The guy took the kids and left his shepherds. But there was heat on him now, so he threw the kids out of his car somewhere in New Jersey and kept right on going, maybe to California. Jack had sold each kid for fifty dollars. Less than people pay for a German shepherd.

Jack is grinning at me now. He knows I am not about to do anything. There's a cop across the street at the Boys' Club.

The two chicks are innocence personified. They're new

in this city. They keep looking at Jack's flowing red hair and his beautiful face—they think he's the greatest guy alive. God only knows how many have thought so before them.

My son runs up to me with a whole bunch of children from PS 122. I embrace him and greet his friends, and we all go to the playground. I have to get that heavy feeling out of my heart.

As I walk away with the kids, I tell Jack a quiet "farewell" in Russian. I don't think he heard me.

A few days later, Jeffrey phones me and tells me excitedly that Jack's been shot and killed. Cops said he was resisting a mugger. It's in the *Daily News*. And so it is. Another hippie murdered, how horrible. When will it all stop?

Jack sure was no hippie. But if the cops determined he was killed by a mugger, that's good enough for me.

I'll believe anything once or twice.

What I won't believe is that there are right now at least ten other Jacks, all colors and all creeds, doing their thing right here in the East Village.

Ridiculous!

A few miles from Scranton, Pennsylvania, the gravel-top country road runs up and down through the hills, skips over some brooks, makes a few turns, and climbs up the hill. My old Studebaker runs surprisingly well. On top of one of the larger hills stands an old Russian church. Behind it a small cemetery, a few wooden buildings, and a large barn. The church was originally built by the Yugoslavian immigrants around the end of the last century. They were followed by the Slovenians and, more recently, by the small Russian congregation headed by a typical Russian village priest called Seraphim. Father Seraphim remembers the red-haired Ivan very well and fondly.

"Ivan was a good boy when his parents were alive. Did you know his mother was Chinese? That's where he got those eyes. Ivan was eleven when he went to live with his sister in Scranton. Oh, his father and mother were already

Once There Was a Village

dead. He lived right here, behind the church and helped me tend the farm. He was a very clever boy. Yes, very clever.

"Not many people want to be buried here," Father Seraphim muses. "They all go to St. Vladimir's Cemetery or to Spring Valley. This is the first burial I've had this year."

The day is getting grayer, unfriendlier. A white wooden Orthodox cross is on top of Jack. Old Slavic letters say, "God have mercy upon the soul of your slave, Ivan————. 1952-1972."

Maybe I am insane. I too say, "God have mercy," and I cross myself.

Pray Kunak, in a foreign country.
Pray Kunak, for your native land.
(from a Russian song)

The word *Kunak* was introduced into mid-nineteenth-century Russia by Shamil, the great leader of Moslem tribes who inhabited the Caucasian mountains. They revolted against Czarist rule and were never conquered ("pacified" was the term then) by the Russian army. Shamil himself was eventually taken prisoner. By that time, everyone in Russia knew of his heroic exploits. He was the most romantic hero Russia ever had, even though he was the enemy of the empire and a pagan in the eyes of the Russian Church. When captured, Shamil was accorded honorable treatment and then exiled. In his exile, he prayed for his proud people. From his famous prayer, immortalized in many great poems and songs, the word *kunak* became a part of Russian and Ukrainian languages.

Kunak means brother, cousin, any relative, someone from your village, a friend you grew up with, a man from your part of the country—almost any man you happen to like. Kunak is also a popular family name among the peasants and the coal-miners of the southern Ukraine, in the region of Donbas.

Oleg Kunak was born on October 1, 1954, in a tenement on Avenue D between Seventh and Eighth Streets. His father, at the time, worked as a furniture mover for Kashtan Brothers. His mother, a small, devoutly religious woman, possessed the priceless skill of Ukrainian needlework and embroidery—an inherited skill, jealously guarded and carefully passed along from generation to generation. Ukrainian needlework is truly a great art. And there were no more than a handful of women in the world capable of creating the designs Oleg's mother Anna was quietly embroidering in her tiny room in the sixth-floor walkup.

Once There Was a Village

Oleg was their only child. Oleg's mother was seldom out of work. Most Ukrainians in the East Village were dirt poor, but there were enough of them who'd rather save a hundred dollars for one of Anna's blouses or shirts than for a new stove or an icebox. There simply wasn't anything so beautiful in America, perhaps not even in the Ukraine. Rumor had it that there was one other woman in Toronto who was Anna's equal. Maybe so.

Vostochnaya Derevnia—the East Village, as it had been called by the Slavs since 1905—was in many ways different in the mid-1950s and in many ways exactly the same. It was a ghetto and an oppressive slum. It was somewhat cleaner, though not nearly as clean as some old residents will tell you. There was very little crime—burglaries were almost unheard of. There were street gangs, however, and these gangs were tough and vicious. The only good thing about them was that they fought one another and left other people in the neighborhood pretty much alone.

Around the time Oleg was eight, heroin was already the coming thing.

About this time, his father fell in love with an American woman and abandoned them.

Anna, who was no more than forty at the time, suddenly looked much older. She was still a beautiful woman with a young girl's figure but the black hair falling down to her waist began turning gray. And her hazel eyes, large, gay, and mischievous, now had traces of weariness and fear.

She didn't cry much when her husband left them. But she was very upset when she learned he had taken all of their savings—almost four thousand dollars, with which they were planning to buy a house in Patterson, New Jersey, and which was mostly her money anyway.

When it rains, it rains hard. A few months later, Oleg was coming home from St. Yuri's parochial school when three Puerto Rican boys jumped him on the stairs of his house.

They mistook Oleg for one of the members of a rival Ukrainian gang and beat him up very badly. Knocked out three of his new teeth, broke his right hand and one of his ribs. He had to go to the hospital.

God only knows what went on in Anna's head. And God wasn't welcome in her house any more.

Anna took all her ikons down from the walls. The ikons she had kissed every day of her life, every evening, every morning. The ikons which used to hang on the walls of her house in her native village, even during the great famine of 1933. The ikons she saved during the war. Her family's ikons. She wrapped them all in a clean white sheet and took them to a Ukrainian dealer who specialized in religious articles. She didn't haggle over the price he offered (which was next to nothing); she barely forced herself to pick up the money and leave the store. That same day she rented a smaller apartment around the corner, on Seventh Street, in a mostly Ukrainian tenement building.

A few uneventful years ran by. Oleg and Anna lived quietly in their cheerful, spotless apartment filled with plants, overstuffed chairs, a couch with dozens of small embroidered pillows on top of it, and a large TV console which didn't work very well.

Outside their apartment, things were changing. The narrow stairs were being swept less and less frequently. People began holding their breath going downstairs, past the dogshit and bags filled with rotting garbage, around a broken icebox which someone left on the stairway, past pried-open mailboxes and half-burnt mattresses by the entrance. And occasionally during the night, people would hear a loud crash—another apartment door being kicked in. Or hear a scream for help—another mugging. All kinds of drugs were flowing in now. And heroin was definitely king.

At thirteen Oleg stopped going to St. Yuri's. He went to P.S. 71 for half a year and then dropped out. Yet his mother never suspected it because Oleg kept bringing home fake report cards, and filling his room with textbooks and books he stole from the Tompkins Square Library.

1968-69 was the time of greatest change on Oleg's block. Street gangs disappeared. Crowds of hippies came in. Many Slavic and Puerto Rican families moved out. Kids began hanging out together, in small groups, usually kids from the same house or the same part of the block. Oleg was now a tall, friendly teenager with curly black hair, a little mustache, and the beginnings of a goatee. He was hanging around with a group of kids from his house and from the house next door. There were two other Ukrainian kids, Tommy and George, a black kid, Nicholas, two Puerto Rican kids, Sammy and Danny, and two girls: Tina, a dark-haired and beautiful Ukrainian, and Sally, an Irish girl, blonde and chubby. The guys were all around fifteen, except for Danny, who was almost seventeen. Both girls were fourteen. They had everything in common. Danny was the only one who lived with his father. The rest lived with mothers or aunts. Not one of them went to school anymore. They were all through with speed, acid, and sex, and were beginning to pick up on heroin. Heroin was very cheap then. You could buy it everywhere. And it was very strong.

Oleg was the last one to shoot up. He was afraid and kept stalling. He kept drinking Thunderbird all day. It was snowing like hell. The empty apartment where they were holding their party was almost hot. All the radiators were hissing. They were burning incense which the hippies who previously had the apartment had left behind. Everyone was spaced out. Oleg was one who was simply drunk. Tina was dancing around and singing. She tried blowing Nicholas and George, but they couldn't get a hard-on. She moved to Oleg. He couldn't make it either.

He thought of his mother, two flights above them, sitting by her old television set, ruining her beautiful eyes. He remembered the time long, long ago when he and his father took the subway to Queens to watch a soccer game between

New York Ukrainians and a visiting German team. It was a tough, exciting game and the Ukrainians beat the hell out of the Germans 7 to 3. It was now dark outside and dark in the apartment. The snow was falling heavily, in huge wet lumps. The block was completely covered. Garbage, abandoned cars, everything.

Oleg was unaware of what was happening in the room. He was feeling very sorry for himself. He felt like praying. He prayed. And as he prayed, he began crying. There was so much he wanted for his mother, for himself. He wanted to buy her a house with a large garden. And for himself, he wanted a car and maybe some job which paid lots of money. He thought he might even get married and have two kids, a boy and a girl. He'd take good care of his family. He'd make sure of that.

Tina came over again and sat on the mattress next to him. This time she had the shit ready. She jabbed him gently in his thigh and soon the apartment became even warmer. The walls opened up, the sky was blue, and everything Oleg wished for became a reality.

This was their last party. Their graduation party. After it, they split up in order to survive.

Oleg and Sammy went into ripping off apartments. Nicholas stole his uncle's pistol and pulled some holdups. Tommy began stealing bikes around NYU. George died from an overdose. Both girls started hustling, working Puerto Rican social clubs and around Union Square.

Nicholas was the first to get caught. It was the stupidest thing, too. He had just ripped off a white musician for forty-five bucks and a wristwatch and was running happily downstairs followed by howls of "Help, police. Nigger, motherfucker, shit, monkey . . ." and so on. (The musician was a true liberal; and he moved to Greenwich Village the next day.) And as Nicholas was making the first flight of stairs, three cops were entering the building. Something so freaky. It never happened before or after. Nicholas had barely enough time to turn around and run back up. Only he couldn't go all the way up—the musician was still screaming on the fourth floor and people were opening doors. So he climbed out of the hall window and jumped across a small shaft to the roof of Finast Supermarket, one floor below. The roof was covered with broken bottles and mounds of garbage. Nicholas fell down hard as he landed. He felt such terrible pain in his legs he almost passed out. He couldn't move one inch. He bit through his lips to keep from screaming. But the cops spotted him anyway and eventually figured out a way to get him off the roof.

By that time, Nicholas was unconscious from pain and loss of blood. He had a broken heel and both his legs were torn wide open. He couldn't even get rid of his gun, his two knives, his needle, and two bags of shit he was going to use later in the evening.

Tommy, the bicycle thief, was caught twice. And twice he was lucky. The cops who grabbed him only took away the bikes and Tommy's bolt cutters and let him loose. And both times, it so happened, Tommy had new fifteen-speed Peugeot racers.

Both Tina and Sally were picked up many times, but they were never booked, never even brought to the Ninth Precinct. They were always released, usually after blowing the cops in their patrol cars or letting the cops fuck them in the East River Park. Sometimes the cops would even give them cigarettes.

Danny, the older kid who lived with his father, was the only one to completely stop using heroin. His father, a tall, stern-looking man who worked as a night watchman, discovered Danny shooting up one morning when he came home a couple of hours earlier than usual. He knocked Danny out with his nightstick, tied him to a drainpipe in his kitchen, stuffed his mouth with old rags and, for three days in a row, he beat Danny mercilessly, using his stick, the

Once There Was a Village

dog chain, and a cast-iron frying pan. On the fourth day, he called the ambulance and Danny was taken to Bellevue. Danny recovered in two months and never touched shit again. He also never went back to his father. For a while, he lived with his aunt in Brooklyn. The last anyone heard he was in the Air Force.

Oleg and Sammy became a very successful team.

The first thirty or so apartments they hit were in the East Village. They were cleaning these apartments the usual way: breaking in the door, knocking out the locks, bending the gates, climbing down the rope, or cutting through the wall from an adjoining empty apartment, all of which were dangerous.

They had quite a few narrow escapes. Twice Oleg was almost pushed out of the window. They were chased by the dogs and the owners, and, one night, even by the cops. They themselves were ripped off on a roof by a group of other junkies and nearly killed. And the merchandise they were getting wasn't worth very much.

Besides, the fence at the liquor store wouldn't buy anything from them after they brought in a stereo and a TV set belonging to a friend of the fence who lived only three houses down from the liquor store on Seventh Street. The friend recognized his stuff and threatened to put them both in jail. It cost Oleg and Sammy their last hundred bucks just to shut him up.

And that's when Oleg decided to start using his brains.

He and Sammy had a great advantage over other junkies. They both had low tolerance for heroin. Sammy was perfectly happy on four bags a day and never went over five. Oleg never went over eight. So they didn't have to run around like a pair of hungry wolves. One good apartment could support them for three or four days. Oleg began cultivating an old Ukrainian locksmith on Ninth Street who knew his mother. Soon Oleg learned to pick almost any lock. He also found out about a new product on the market: a high-speed, battery-operated hacksaw that could cut an inch-thick steel bar in less than a minute, and quietly.

It also became clear to Oleg that if they continued operating around Avenues B and C, they'd be either in jail, in a hospital, or dead. Within a few weeks.

They had still another advantage over most junkies. They were a pair of hippie-looking white teenagers, handsome, well-dressed, and well-behaved. Exactly the kind of kids you'd see in good neighborhoods like Brooklyn Heights or the West Village. And it was to these two neighborhoods Oleg and Sammy shifted their operation.

By comparison, it was like taking candy from a baby. And it was the sweetest candy they had ever tasted. No one paid them the slightest attention. One afternoon, for example, Oleg was coming out of the house they had just cleaned out on West Eleventh Street with a portable color TV in one hand, a tape recorder in another, wearing a leather coat which he had also taken, with three expensive cameras dangling under it. He walked right past a parked squad car to the VW bus he and Sammy had stolen the night before, and they drove off. The cops never turned heads in their direction.

They also masqueraded as a pair of homosexuals. Who'd suspect a gay couple of being ripoffs?

As they prospered, they rented a ground-floor apartment with two entrances in a safe Slavic building on Third Street just off Second Avenue. And they made it impenetrable. They each had a room. The large room in the back became their warehouse.

They told their mothers they had jobs and showered them with expensive gifts. Oleg gave his mother a color TV set and a new sewing machine, among other things. He remembered to take his mother to a good eye doctor, and just in time too. She had glaucoma and otherwise would have been totally blind within a year. The one thing they didn't tell their mothers was their address and exactly where they worked. And they never ever invited anyone to their pad. On their mailbox were two new and innocent

names. Instead of Oleg Kunak, there was now Al Cook.
Instead of Sammy Lopez, there was S. Long.

The owner of the building thought they were students.
The deaf Ukrainian super thought they were great
gentlemen—at least once a month, they'd give the old man
five bucks to buy himself some vodka.

Sometimes they'd run into Tina or Sally, who now
worked out of a rooming house on Third Avenue. Tina was
still good-looking, but Sally was getting ugly. She was heavy
and her face was covered by a mass of pimples.

Oleg saw Tommy a few times and even bought a bike
from him. Tommy was hanging around Astor Place. He
told Oleg he had stolen over five hundred bikes by now,
which was probably true. Still, Tommy didn't look very
good—his beautiful sealskin jacket was torn and dirty, his
face was also covered by pimples, and he had a deep scar
across his forehead. It was harder and harder for him to
steal. He was beginning to LOOK like a junkie.

While Oleg and Sammy had the VW bus, they sometimes
worked out on Long Island. One afternoon, driving back
through Queens (they avoided main highways as much as
possible), they went right past the small Ukrainian cemetery
where George had been buried. They had all been surprised when George died. George was the healthiest of the
bunch. He was always happy, too, and always kidding
around. Oleg and Tommy both attended his funeral at St.
Yuri's Cathedral. It was a fine funeral. The priest didn't
even know George died from an overdose. Later that day,
Oleg gave George's mother, Pelageja, an almost new Tele-
funken short-wave radio set so she could listen to Ukrainian
and Russian programs. Oleg didn't think he'd ever see
George's grave, but since they were right here and the
cemetery gates were wide open, he drove in.

Sammy stayed in the bus while Oleg went to find the
grave.

It wasn't hard to find; the cemetery was very small.

George's grave was in the last row, near the fence. It was drizzling. The grave was muddy and forlorn. There was a bunch of dried flowers on it. Almost all the white paint had peeled off George's wooden cross. Next to George's grave was a fresh grave with a new stone cross and a large wreath of chrysanthemums. George's mother Pelageja. She had outlived her son by almost a year. Oleg wondered who got her radio. It was worth at least seventy bucks.

This was a strange fucked-up afternoon. Sammy was in a rotten mood, nagging about a Polaroid camera Oleg forgot to take. Oleg worried whether they had enough gas to make it back.

As soon as they got the merchandise into their apartment and bolted the doors, they went to their rooms and shot up. Oleg thought it was taking him forever to get high. He was worried about this and that. Sure, he thought, the back room is still waist-high with good, fast merchandise, but how long can we keep it up? And Sammy is getting to be a real stupid bitch. That reminded Oleg. He walked to Sammy's room and knocked. Sammy didn't answer. Oleg stopped in the back room to count the stuff they'd picked up in Smithtown. Sure enough. There should've been two rifles, three shotguns, and a real cowboy gunbelt with two Colt .45's in the sack. One of the Colts had six notches on it. The Colts and the rifles were there, but one of the shotguns was missing.

Oleg checked the jewelry chest. Half of the jewelry was missing. He counted the wristwatches. Four, maybe five were missing. He looked around the room. Something else was missing. But he was feeling much better now. He went back to his room and put two Ukrainian records on. He looked at his beautiful Ukrainian shirt which his mother had given him for his seventeenth birthday the week before, which he had hung over his bed so he could groove on it every time he came back. He was amazed at the patterns, at all the work involved. Everytime he looked at the designs, he discovered something new. How could she do it? How could anyone make something so beautiful? With just some thread and a few needles?

And then he laughed and laughed.

I am also making beautiful things with my needle. And my needle is beautiful too! He really did have a beautiful, Swiss-made syringe—he had given fifteen bucks for it to the junkies who had ripped off a truckload of hospital supplies.

"My needle is so beautiful," he sang. He flipped the records over. There was one song he especially loved. He had sung it at the school concert in honor of the Ukrainie's greatest poet Taras Shevchenko:

> *I look at the sky, and I have but one thought,*
> *Why am I not a falcon, why can't I fly?*
> *Why couldn't God give me wings?*
> *I'd leave this world and soar higher than the*
> *   clouds . . .*

That had been a great concert. The Bishop himself shook Oleg's hand. That was his last year at St. Yuri's. They had no more money and the school wouldn't keep him. His grades were just average. His mother begged the principal, but he wouldn't let Oleg stay.

That was the same year he had to take his mother to the welfare offices and translate all the bullshit questions they asked her. And when she broke down and cried, the stupid social worker thought she was crazy. He told Oleg maybe she should go to a hospital.

Something was still wrong; he was still worried. He was coming down too fast. He shot up another bag. That was all he needed. That felt great.

The next morning he knew exactly what he had to do. He had to get rid of Sammy. That motherfucker, bitching about one fucking camera. Oleg was furious. He'll fuck up for sure. He doesn't know shit about selling—who to see, what to ask. He might even sell to an undercover pig. He's a good thief, and that's all, bro. And what's this shit about being even, always even? Where the fuck did the watches go, and the jewelry? He'll fuck up! He'll fuck up and with all the merchandise we have here, I'll get maybe ten years.

Going to jail was the only thing Oleg was afraid of. He'd much rather be dead.

That evening they cleaned out a photographer's loft in Chelsea. They stored all the equipment safely in the back room and then were just two happy little kids. Very, very happy, and at least a couple of thousand bucks richer. They embraced each other, danced, drank some wine, shot up, talked about splitting New York, going to California or even Hawaii. About the new white whore they both had tried who was unbelievable—the guy only had to stick his dick in, front or back, and hold it there, and it didn't even have to be that hard, and she'd lay there and work her muscles and in less than thirty seconds the guy would be spraying his head off and yelling with joy. And they talked about Seventh Street, how they were stealing car batteries whenever it rained. How they tried getting a new icebox out of their super's basement, and the super chasing them with an ax.

Now Tommy was in Bernstein, the lucky sonofabitch. But then Tommy was always lucky. Sally got cut up by some creep and died. Tina was hustling up in Harlem. Nicholas was out for a while. Then he dropped out of sight. Probably back in jail somewhere. And Danny boy is flying, really flying.

And they? They had made it big. They had everything. All the shit they could use. All the bread. And in the big room, in the back, five portable color TV sets. Thousands of dollars of other merchandise: cameras, tape recorders, electric typewriters, stereos, black-and-white TV sets, film equipment, darkroom equipment, anything.

They were grooving together that night. Spaced out, they embraced and fell asleep together on the same bed in Sammy's room.

In the morning, it was another story. They were both wary. Sammy sensed Oleg's anger. They kept their hands close to their knives. They knew each other only too well. And they watched each other like a pair of stray cats.

Later that night they drove back to Long Island. There was one house they knew, begging to be cleaned out. It was to be the last time for the VW bus. It was repainted and had stolen Vermont plates on it; still they had had it for four months. It was getting too risky to keep it any longer.

Oleg drove, as usual. That's one thing Sammy had never learned, how to drive. Oleg turned off the Southern Parkway and without slowing down, stabbed Sammy hard in the neck and twisted his knife as he pulled it out.

Sammy screamed, coughed, and choked. He pulled out his own knife, but it was too late. Oleg held the bus steady with his left hand and stabbed Sammy in his side a couple of times to make sure. He didn't have to do it; Sammy was gone.

It was around one in the morning.

No traffic.

Oleg stopped in a deserted wooded area, took everything out of Sammy's pockets and put them in his shoulder bag. Sammy was bleeding like a pig. Oleg opened the door and grabbed Sammy's body, being careful not to get too much blood on him. He carried Sammy down the slope. Sammy was so light. He rolled him under thick blackberry bushes, way out of sight, and wiped his hands and his jacket on the wet grass. Then he drove to Stony Brook, parked the VW bus near the college campus, stole a black '64 Ford, and drove it back.

He got back to Third Street about two thirty. Now he wasn't worried. He felt happy even before he shot up. In the apartment next door, a Ukrainian family was having one of their noisy parties. Oleg lay on his bed and half-listened to the muted sounds coming through the wall. He shot two extra bags just to be on the safe side. He got up and checked the merchandise. Now everything was here, and every fuckin' thing was his.

One thing bugged him a little. The last time he had visited his mother she had asked him point-blank whether he was a junkie. Why would she even think of that? Oleg wondered and dismissed it from his mind. He was feeling no pain.

The Ukrainians next door were dancing and laughing and singing sad songs about love and their homeland; somebody was playing the accordion.

Oleg felt great. He sang quietly too. He covered himself with his beautiful Ukrainian shirt and stroked the embroidered patterns. He knew God had given him wings.

He was soaring higher and higher. Higher than he'd ever flown before.

Higher than God Himself.

Oleg is serving six months on Rikers Island right now. I don't know exactly what for.

I heard a lot of wild stories about him recently. It seems he went heavily into the moving business with some oldtime hoods. They were stealing moving vans in New Jersey, then driving to some estate in upper New York and moving everything of value from that estate. And on one or two occasions, they were chased by the cops with everybody shooting at each other, ramming the truck through roadblocks, overturning, running into forests, being chased by the dogs and, after being caught, breaking out of some county jail by taking the sheriff as a hostage at knifepoint. Would you believe? I would, it's a real American adventure—to be continued, I am sure, after Oleg gets out.

Tommy got out of Bernstein and was stabbed to death in a fight about a month later. Nicholas was wounded in the Attica uprising and transferred to some other jail. Tina died—I don't know the circumstances surrounding her death.

Oleg's mother is still alive, living in the same apartment. She was mugged three times and once badly beaten up by one of the muggers. She is in poor health.

Danny is back in Puerto Rico. He is married, has a year-old son and a good job. A few days ago, I was at a party on my old block. The guy who gave it showed me the photograph Danny sent him: Danny with his wife, holding his son in front of their new house. It was a small house in a Spanish style, and there was a palm tree by the side of the house. That palm really freaked me out. I want a house like that with a palm tree.

Danny was the only one of these kids who "made it."

Once There Was a Village

The Saturday Night Special, as everyone knows or should know by now, is usually a .22-caliber revolver, very cheaply made—in my case, by a company on Long Island called Triumph. I've seen BB pistols better made. Still, it was kind of cute, and the bullets were real enough. The white plastic handle looked a lot better when I borrowed my son's flat black Tensor paint and painted it black.

Most Saturday Night Specials, including mine, are bought down in the Carolinas for about fifteen dollars or less along with a box of bullets and brought back to New York in cars or buses. It should be noted that these Specials are resold in New York for two and three times their price in the South.

These Specials serve well two main purposes for which they are bought: one, to hold up something or somebody, and two, to protect someone from being held up. There are probably more Saturday Night Specials in New York City than anybody imagines. I know for a fact that all kids on my block from sixteen on up own Specials (Puerto Rican kids, black and white kids, too). They don't have them necessarily for mugging but rather to keep themselves from being ripped off. There's another reason for guns, too. The guns are very closely related to the drug culture and they are an extension of the kids' manhood, taken very seriously, just like friendships or shooting the first bag.

Most Saturday Night Specials are used sooner or later, and some are used a lot sooner than their owners wish or expect.

In the fall of '71, the mugging situation between Avenues B and D became even worse than that in the spring of '69. Now the sweet early days of mugging, when muggers were satisfied with a purse or a wallet, were over. Now they'd force the victim into his or her apartment and clean it out, and sometimes they hurt the victim or victims before leaving. I don't know what happened on the Upper West Side or in some other section of the city; all of a sudden we had a huge influx of muggers and junkies which no one had ever seen before. Vicious gutter rats. Crowds of them stood on Eleventh Street near Avenue B on a twenty-four-hour basis, waiting for their dealers. Tompkins Square Park was flooded by them; every doorway on Ninth Street between B and D had clusters of junkies and ripoffs hanging out like hungry vultures. The People's Park on Seventh Street, the whole of Seventh Street, was crowded with types I wouldn't want to meet even on a bright sunny day. And forget the knives. This new wave had Saturday Night Specials, Magnums, sawed-off shotguns. One cat I knew slightly even carried a grenade in his shoulderbag.

It wasn't so much a choice with me as it was a necessity. I had to get a gun just to live through the winter.

Now buying a gun in New York was out of the question. For pitiful-looking weapons, people were paying seventy, eighty, even a hundred bucks. I was broke, as usual. I had a very good friend, though, a young actress who went down South from time to time.

Besides, in New York when you buy a used gun, you don't know what you're getting. Ten people could've been killed with it and you won't know about it until you get busted.

My friendly actress was a gutsy, down-to-earth chick. I mentioned the need for a gun. She said she'd get it for me and she got it—a present—my shiny, cheap Triumph plus a box of bullets. That first day I felt like a kid with a new toy, a forbidden toy, which made it even more exciting.

Quite a long time ago, while I was in the army, stationed at Fort Knox, Kentucky, I bought myself a .22-caliber rifle. I only shot it a few times in the forest. The rifle was lost somewhere and I never missed it. Good thing too, because during one of our stormy fights, my wife probably would've shot me with it.

Now I had my Triumph revolver. Seven tiny bullets went into it. The cheap white plastic handle became black and better-looking. I showed it off to some friends, and put it under my mattress, where it lay for a couple of weeks except for three or four times when I went to a bar late at night.

On that fateful day, December 2, 1971—I should've read the *Daily News* horoscope—it said that Pisceans should not

Once There Was a Village

go out of the house that day—a friend stopped by with his newly acquired gun. His was a better gun than mine, also .22-caliber but made in Germany, with a long barrel.

We went out looking for a place to try out our revolvers. He shot his in one of the basements—too loud. We finally went into an empty storefront. He shot his a few times and I shot mine once. I am a reasonably good shot and was awarded some kind of cross for it in the army during my basic training. I shot once and I hit the middle of a piece of paper we were shooting at. Which is roughly equivalent to shooting a bulls-eye in darts. I didn't have the time to stick around and shoot a few more times. I was already late—my son was playing with one of his friends and I knew that by themselves they'd play pretty wild and I had to start cooking supper anyway.

I quickly reloaded the gun, threw it in my shoulderbag, and went home.

It was dark as I was approaching my house and cold. I noticed a junkie whom I had never seen before leaning on the fence of the parking lot, checking out the windows. I went past him, crossed the street to my entrance. He crossed the street after me. I wasn't worried; the junkie very seldom operates alone. They usually run in bunches of two, three, and four—gives them more courage. Before entering my building, I turned around to face him, just in case. Then something happened which I didn't expect; there were two of them. The second guy was hiding behind the cars and jumped out at the last minute.

And there he is, I am looking at two of them now. The one who was hiding has his knife out. A perfect setup. I don't know how I missed it! I am in the corner near our door so I can't come out into the street and call my friends and I also can't go into the building. If I do, that would be the end.

I tell the junkie with the knife to put it away. I have my hand on my gun in my shoulderbag which I am holding in front of me. I tell them I have a piece, one more step, one more move, and I'll first shoot their legs from under them.

They look at my hand in my bag and they're cooled off. The main thing in muggings is speed. Even if I didn't have the gun in my bag, they would have backed off. The element of surprise is gone and they're not yet in the building. They're angry! They say something like "Shit, you ain't got nothing, put your shit away, you wanna fight?" But they don't move toward me, not one inch.

It's the classic East Village standoff. I wait another minute or so. They back off a little. It's really the end of that encounter. I take my gun from my shoulder bag and put it in my pocket to make sure I've got it if they decided to follow me. Then I go into my building.

The next thing that happened was totally unheard-of. Two patrolmen were hurrying along Seventh Street to investigate a dispute (a what?) and the junkies, still in front of my house and seeing the cops so unexpectedly, freaked out, jumped around, and yelled, "He has a gun, that guy has a gun," pointing to me as I was trying to open the inner door. One chance in a million—two cops on Seventh Street at five in the evening. Then another chance in a million—my key gets stuck in the door. All the years I've lived here and it never happened. It had to happen that night.

And the cops freaked out too. They ran after me, placed one of their huge guns to my temple, another to my heart, yelled at me, and went through my pockets. Since I had my gun right in my pocket, they found it.

In the meantime, both junkies slipped their knives into our garbage can (a kid from my building retrieved both knives the next morning when he took down the garbage). But the junkies couldn't simply run off now. All of a sudden, the street became covered with cops and squad cars.

As I was being dragged from my doorway, I said, "Look, what about these two ripoffs? I live here, what the fuck were they doing here?" So one of the cops invited them to come along, which they happily agreed to do since they were now clean.

The junkies were soon released. One of them turned out

to be only sixteen, less than a month out of Bernstein Institute (most of Bernstein is a methadone hospital). They said they were brothers, which was just as much bullshit as the addresses they gave the cops. One of them was supposed to show up in court the next day—he didn't. In fact, the judge was ready to issue the warrant for his arrest when I told him I didn't want to prosecute anybody—jail is the worst place for the addict.

The Ninth Precinct must have been built in the late nineteenth century—a dreary, slimy, dirty "reception hall," right out of some James Cagney movie. Fat, slimy-looking lieutenants and sergeants staring down at me—"What do we have here?"—projecting their sick minds: "You got the gun so you could go out and kill cops, right?" Smell of urine, vomit, and sweat. In the back it's much worse. Their cell block is from the Middle Ages. Reminded me of one Dracula flick where Drac had the job of a prison warden.

By the time I was locked up in my cell, a few things were cleared up. Like the fact that I wasn't going anywhere. And, yes, they allowed me to make one phone call and I called a friend who took care of the kids and notified my other friends of my misfortune. Now I wasn't worried about anyone except myself. The cops were very explicit and kept telling me over and over again that under New York's Sullivan Law, I was facing two to five. I always thought the penalty was high, but I had had no idea it was that high. As it turned out, it wasn't, but that night I was convinced I'd get around six months, four months with good behavior.

Serves you right, stupid, I thought. You shouldn't have stood there, should've blown both junkies away, run to the roof, thrown the gun into our chimney, and that would have been the end of the story. And their ghosts would've never haunted me, either. I've seen so many people killed during the war and, come to think of it, right here in the East Village. It wouldn't have bothered my conscience one bit. Only it was needless. Why should I kill the junkies anyway? I was finished with them and they were finished with me. There was no more "dispute." And, besides, I am an artist, not a killer. A while back, I even swore off killing cockroaches.

The hell of it was when I saw the cops running toward me I should've thrown my gun away immediately. Only where could I throw it? Our vestibule (as the judge later kindly called it) is a five-foot by four-foot enclosure big enough only for our mailboxes. If only my key hadn't stuck. I should've been carrying my knife instead of a gun. Although who knows, maybe things worked out for the better. I didn't see the second guy after all until it was almost too late. With only one knife against two, I might have gotten myself killed. Anyway, there's not one thing I can do about it now.

It was around eight o'clock. I sat on a bench and was thinking unhappy thoughts when a cop came in with some sandwiches and an opened can of Coca-Cola. No, they don't feed anybody at the Ninth Precinct. It was my friend, the actress, feeling somewhat remorseful about having given me the gun, who had stopped by the stationhouse, and in that Coca-Cola can was actually some good rum which she infused there. She had also made the sandwiches. That rum was what I needed. In my shoulderbag, along with my sketchpad, I had half a pint of Canadian Club. My shoulderbag was behind their front desk and the last time they showed it to me, there was no Canadian Club in there. And there was no sketchpad either. I never got these two items back.

It did not seem illogical at all for me to be in jail. Some of the best people I've known were busted at one time or another for one reason or another and sometimes for no reason at all. At least there's no denying I had a piece on me. All things considered, I'd rather go through this shit than be recovering from stab wounds in a place like Bellevue with my family and friends visiting me and crying by my bedside as the intravenous solution drips slowly. Drip, drip.

Around one in the morning, a sweet-looking sergeant stopped by my cell and talked to me. I don't know whether

Once There Was a Village

he was pumping me or not. If he was, he didn't do such a good job. I was in no mood to talk. The sergeant told me a brief history of the Ninth Precinct jail—used to be mostly Irish and Italians who sat there, real mad dogs too, both of them, the cops were even afraid to search them. Then it was Poles; now it's mostly Puerto Ricans. They still get blacks and Poles and hippie types, but mostly it's Puerto Rican addicts. Ninth Precinct, the portals into American life.

According to the sergeant, I had nothing to worry about. Everybody carries guns in New York City. I should just tell the judge where I live and he'll understand. I thought to myself, "Sure, kid, sure. And Santa too will come down my chimney this Christmas."

Around 2:00 A.M. there was a big hassle in the hall. Two cops pushed a guy into the cell next door to mine. This guy was too drunk to comprehend what was happening. He kept asking the cops who gave them permission to bust into his apartment and what was the charge. The cop who was pushing him most, an unpleasant wise-guy type, told him the charge was "attempted murder, among other things." The guy in the next cell turned out to be Polish. Only after the cops left did I realize what they did to him—they took away his jacket, he only had a shirt on him, and they opened the window in the corridor across from his cell. It was a very cold night. I was shivering in my heavy overcoat and sweater. My feet were freezing. The Polish guy in the next cell was coughing and throwing up and freezing to death. I'd have given him my sweater but there was no way for me to reach him. He was crying and coughing and vomiting the rest of the night. From his broken sentences, in Polish and English, and from his curses, I got a pretty good picture of what had happened to him.

He was a cook and he recently broke up with the love of his life, a waitress. Usually she'd come back to him after a few days. This time she wasn't coming back; there was another man. The guy began drinking. He lost his job. That night he had been drinking and playing his records full blast. His neighbors complained. Two cops knocked on his door. He didn't know they were cops, he grabbed the kitchen knife and opened his door. The cops pushed him into his apartment. He probably made some threatening gestures with his knife and they took it away. They took him away too. He cursed at the cops and they decided to cool him.

The morning finally arrived. We were handcuffed together and the cop who arrested the Polish guy took us to the Tombs. By now the Polish guy was delirious. I can still feel it; he was shaking so hard my hand was jumping up and down. He didn't make any sense now, and every word was followed by a spasm of heavy coughing. He tried vomiting, only nothing was coming out any more. He passed out twice and regained consciousness. He had a hell of a constitution. I almost passed out from the stink of his vomit, all over him.

It seemed we were riding in the paddy wagon for a couple of hours. When we reached the Tombs, the cop opened the door, pushed the Polish guy out first, and as he was pushing him out said, "How do you feel now, motherfucker?" and hit him on the back of his head with a blackjack or something.

In the Tombs we were split up and I never saw the Polish guy again. I hope he's alive. I hope he's free and I hope his woman came back to him.

It was Friday morning at the Tombs. They searched me again and put me in a large bullpen to await my arresting officer, who was then supposed to take me for processing, photos (mugshots), and so forth. Every Friday at the Tombs there's a feeling of special anxiety—no one wants to sit in there through the weekend. So the sooner your cop comes, the better were your chances to go before the judge and possibly be released on bail or probation.

My arresting cop was not a bad guy. In the months that followed and all the appearances before the grand jury and the judges, my lawyer and I and the cop almost became friends. In a very strange way. My cop was certainly not the shit who arrested the Polish guy.

Once There Was a Village

Anyway, my cop arrived early, we went through processing, and I was locked up in another bullpen, a lot smaller, with about forty other people. We were really like sardines in a can. All the seats on the bench were taken; people were sleeping under the bench, sitting on the floor and on the toilet bowl and still there was no room at all. About two guys had to stand and alternate with those who were sitting.

All ages and all groups, ethnic and otherwise, were well represented. There was a white pimp (Upper East Side bartender type), a black pimp, and a Puerto Rican pimp. There was an older white man in a gray business suit (I don't know what he was in for), three black queens, and an immaculately dressed black heroin dealer, the original Superfly—his head was shaved, he was wearing a one-piece stretch burgundy-colored suit with burgundy-colored boots and tan leather midicoat exactly the color of his skin. I learned later that in one of the pockets of that leather coat was a loaded .38 magnum and in another a quarter of a pound of pure heroin. The dealer never spoke a word to the other prisoners and no one spoke to him. There were three white junkies still spaced out who looked like they'd slept in the streets for at least a month and so ridden with lice or some other bugs that the rest of the prisoners tried not to sit too close to them. There was a black kid, a professional thief, who had been kept for three days in some uptown precinct and who hadn't eaten for three days. There were two handsome black kids from Trinidad. They had stolen a car and gone on a wild joyride at more than a hundred miles an hour up and down Riverside Drive and upper Broadway. They sideswiped several cars, including a police car, and were eventually cornered and caught on 137th Street. They looked like they were about twelve, no more. There was an older black man around fifty whose only fault was that he fell asleep in the wrong place—on the Long Island Expressway. He stopped the car on the shoulder of the road; he was so tired he wanted to take a short nap. He forgot to turn the motor off. It was a car he had borrowed from a friend and the friend probably had stolen it. When there was no place in our bullpen for anybody else, in were shoved three Puerto Rican bank-robbers. They were high-class dudes, too. They kept in a bunch by themselves and looked down upon the rest of us.

After I got out, some people were asking me whether there was hostility between white, black, or Puerto Rican prisoners. I didn't see it in our bullpen. People accepted one another on a person-to-person basis and besides, everybody was in trouble. One black guy was bothering the queens for a while, but it wasn't really mean. After several hours, they began taking people out to another bullpen and then before the judge. Late in the afternoon, I got lucky; they took me out, let me speak to a Legal Aid lawyer for about one minute and, in another hour or so, took me before the judge. It took another minute—since I had no previous record, I was let out on probation and my case referred to the grand jury. Which was the beginning of a very long hassle.

When I think about the Tombs and the jammed bullpens and the judges, I can't help but think that such must have been the situation in Russia prior to the revolution, when the empire began to crack up. Only here the empire doesn't seem to be cracking up yet. It's just sitting there on top of thousands of people caught in its so-called judicial process. And these people don't mean a thing. And it's racist, too —the majority of people busted are black and Puerto Rican (although whites are beginning to make inroads into jails once again), and the majority of the judges are white. You figure it out.

I went before the grand jury with my story. That's sort of like being on the stage with questions from the audience (jurors) and the district attorney. The DA stands way up on the top of the coliseum in the last row and asks questions like "You did have a gun, didn't you?"

"And it was loaded, wasn't it?"

"And why didn't you apply for a permit?"

Actually, I did call the Ninth Precinct to find out how to go about getting a permit. The cop I spoke to choked laughing at me.

"Are you really an artist?"

Questions like that. So it's not exactly simply telling the jury your side of the story and letting them decide. It's the district attorney's show all the way.

My case was reduced to a misdemeanor and sent to Criminal Court.

Another couple of judges, my case kept getting adjourned. Then, this summer, I went before a very unusual judge. I was sitting in his courtroom almost falling asleep and then I began listening. The judge actually cared about the people who came before him. He took his time with the defendants, listened to their stories, talked to their mothers, their relatives. I could tell he liked people and he wasn't just sitting there to pronounce sentences.

When my turn came, Bob, my attorney, advanced the idea that the evidence, the gun, should be suppressed. A question of constitutional rights.

What if the cops start grabbing everyone pointed out to them as having a gun? Bob thought there should be some kind of procedure, to say the least. Bob can argue much better than I can write, but this was the question in a nutshell. The judge called me to the witness stand and let me tell my story once more. As I sat in the witness box and I looked at the judge—he was black—I knew that if there was any way he could help me, he'd find it. There's a feeling when two men look very closely at one another and they both know exactly what the story is and there is almost no need to speak or argue. The judge got the picture, all of it, even before I opened my mouth.

He was frankly pessimistic about his ruling in favor of Bob's motion, but he said he'd give it some thought.

A month later, another appearance. Only two minutes, no more. The judge was too busy. He said that while he types only with one finger, he researches with both eyes. He handed his decision to the DA and Bob, and said simply that the motion to suppress was granted.

This astounded the DA, who took off and rubbed his

thick glasses—the next best thing to rubbing his ears. When I had walked into the court that morning, the DA greeted me in Russian and said something else to me in Russian. Unfortunately, I was too tired to be impressed. The decision astounded Bob, but most of all, it astounded me. I was resigned to pay my dues to society in some way. It was a beautiful decision, though—ten tightly written pages. I think the last paragraph about sums it up. Here it is:

> In the long season of violence which has afflicted America since its entry into World War II and wars around the world, it is a great pity that citizens can come by guns so easily. And, of course, it is to be deplored that the situation of this time surrounds us like a baffling crime, making the streets unsafe and our very homes domestic forts, bristling with locks and hopeful devices to trap the desperate intruder. It is a great pity that the unlicensed peddlers of weapons and narcotics cannot more often be brought to heel. Fair play and the Constitution, however, define limits which, when breached by official zeal, imperil the marking of proofs which indict and convict the guilty.

> > " * * * on a motion to suppress, this court may not Constitutionally accept evidence of defendant's guilt and also close its eyes to the manner in which such evidence was obtained. It is painful at times to be compelled to suppress evidence knowing that a defendant is in fact guilty, but Constitutional requirements make it mandatory upon the court to suppress evidence of guilt obtained in violation of a defendant's Constitutional rights.
> > "This is precisely the situation here. * * *"

Once There Was a Village

[*People v. Mendez*, N. Y. L. I., March 17, 1964, p. 17, Special Term, Queens Sup. Ct., J. Irwin Shapiro (now Associate Justice, App. Div. Second Dept.)]

For the several reasons stated, the motion to suppress is granted.

Bruce McM. Wright

May 12, 1972

The case did not end with this decision. Bob had to appear a few more times, and there was a question of the DA appealing the case and there were other questions. Finally, almost a year later, it was dismissed.

I feel I was very lucky; so many people don't have that kind of luck. They rot in jails, they get bad lawyers and bad judges. They are swallowed or mutilated by the whole system of injustice. My lawyer, Bob Blum—an old friend of Jimmy, my neighbor downstairs—and now my friend—was just great. Bob is a very good chess-player, and I'd like to play with him someday when I am not bartending. I've played him from behind the bar a lot. I don't think that day will be soon, because he's so busy defending so many people, most of whom are political prisoners. He's the new kind of attorney. He knows that today's system of oppression doesn't work, but it's still there and he's confronted with it daily, with all its rotten aspects. But he's bending it as much as he can and chipping at it as much as he can and some fresh air does filter through. Who knows, perhaps one day people like Bob and just plain people will prevail and the system will fall. Someday soon, I hope. And without people resorting to their guns and their Saturday Night Specials.

It's raining today.

Another summer seems to be over in this timeless never-never-land part of the East Village, east of Avenue B.

Instead of heroin, most kids are now taking off on wine and methadone, it's so much cheaper. Coke is still going strong but it's getting harder to get and the quality is bad. Many artists have left and many tenements have been demolished and new co-op towers built in their place. My son now goes to another school, P.S. 20. The leaves in our beautiful backyard are pale yellow and green; they remind me of my butterfly, her hair, her eyes.

I pour the beer and mix the drinks at the Frog Pond. I stand behind the long bar, talk with my customers, and look at the door. I hope she'll fly through it one evening.

Bartending is a rotten job, but I need the bread and I like most of the people who come here. I have a new one-man show at the Educational Alliance; it's just about over. Soon I'll have to take down my new piano constructions and bring them home. At least I was lucky enough to sell one. I'll have to borrow a car somewhere.

So many people are lost, so many are found; so many days and nights and years in this never-never-land still known as the East Village, east of Avenue B.

I suppose the artists will go on painting and starving wherever they happen to be, and the writers will go on writing, and some will do both. A truly creative person is usually not limited to any one activity. Creative talents are so much related and, in the end, so much a part of living —growing roses or growing pot, making a construction, finishing a pen-and-ink, writing a poem, teaching a child. Creativity is considerably stronger than death. Even in the East Village, even today.

Our super, Maria, will take care of our two buildings. She'll shovel coal every night so our ancient stoves will heat our ancient boilers and we'll have enough hot water. She'll keep our buildings clean and look out for us and we'll try to look out for her. She's one of the most beautiful persons I've had the privilege of meeting.

Her rosebushes will bloom again this spring. And when it

gets warm, around Orthodox Easter, we'll all go down into her yard, make a table from one of the thrown-out doors, cover it with a checkered tablecloth, and drink vodka and beer. And eat some of the special Ukrainian dishes she'll cook for the occasion. And Jimmy will play the trumpet or his drums. And my son and Jim's son will play their clarinets. And I'll try to sing some Russian or Ukrainian song. And everybody will scream at me to shut up. And toward the evening we'll be very happy. Like the last year, like the year before.

Jimmy will play in another *Superfly* movie. *Superfly*, by the way, was shot right here on Eleventh Street in our building and in our backyard. And in Jimmy's apartment. Jimmy played a junkie in the beginning of the film. That weird piano-construction on the wall of his apartment was mine, needless to say. What do you know, my work got into a popular movie. And Jimmy will go on doing his plumbing and electrical jobs too. And we both will drink a lot of beer, vodka, gin, Scotch, and bourbon, approximately in that order.

There are thirty-eight tenements on Eleventh Street between Avenues B and C. Four empty lots where children play among the garbage and burnt-out cars. Four abandoned tenements and several semi-abandoned. That is, most of the apartments in them are empty. We have four Puerto Rican social clubs with all the action one might want, and a bar with an American flag sticker on its door and Nixon portraits on the walls. Five tiny groceries are stuck here and there on the block. We even had a restaurant called the Magnolia Coffee Shop across from my tenement, but it folded a few months ago, as the building in which it was located became abandoned.

After the repeal of rent control on newly vacant apartments, our landlords freaked out and began charging $125 or $150 for pitiful three-room apartments in buildings that even dogs are afraid to enter. And that without fixing anything in the apartment or in the building. Our darling governor really put the knife in the backs of people around here with his decontrol. The old people were hit hardest, as usual.

This is probably the major reason why at least a third of all apartments between B and C and Fourteenth Street down to Houston are now empty. Another reason is that many Puerto Rican families are finally moving into the middle class and out of the neighborhood. Then there's still crime and fear of crime. And assorted smaller reasons. One family I knew over the years who used to live on Sixth Street and then on Eleventh Street—mother with three sons, one of whom was my son's classmate—moved to Oregon to work on the farm. Mother believed her kids kept getting sick because of our foul air. They moved about a year ago, and her apartment, in a tenement a few doors from mine, is still empty. And in her former building, which is exactly like mine—five stories, ten apartments—only two families remain. Busted windows on every floor, no heat or hot water, electricity hooked up by an extension cord from another building, and the hallways not swept for months.

The same picture is seen on every block of the East Village, east of Avenue B. Some blocks are nothing but bombed-out ruins. On Seventh Street between B and C, a large tenement across from my old house recently became abandoned. A few stoops away, a Jewish woman who lived there for more than twenty years walked out of her apartment, left everything in it, and left the door open. The kids and "young people" had a field day carrying off her belongings. *Zorba the Greek* and then some. The woman never came back.

And in my old quiet building on Seventh Street, no one has died in the past few years. Mike was the last one to go. The Irish grandmother is finally moving out. Her older grandson is married and has a job in a supermarket. Her younger grandson is back in school. The Puerto Rican family with the baby and black Great Dane who moved into Mike's old apartment is now split up; the Great Dane is dead. Next to my apartment, where the Polish gravedigger used to live a few lifetimes ago, now lives a very nice family with a brand-new baby and a lively dog. The old Spanish man on the top floor is still there. Where else can he go? The Albanians continue moving in, though in smaller numbers. They are "the new wave" and quite probably the last.

My piano construction "The War Is Not Yet Over" seems to be almost obsolete. Just like the East Village. Not quite, but almost. The East Village served its purpose and is no longer needed. And it must die. That's the American way.

A Sunday fire is very bad news. Last Sunday, a beautiful morning, I am taking my son and two of his friends to ride bikes in Tompkins Square Park. They are going to race on all sidewalks, through the playgrounds, and I'll sit in the sun and watch out for ripoffs. Bikes still get ripped frequently. We pull our bikes into the street. A cloud of gray smoke pours out of the window of a building a few doors away. I know what that means. The kids look, curiously. Sounds of broken glass, more smoke, flames jump out from second-floor windows, climb to the third floor. A faint siren. The flames engulf the second floor and push their way into the third. On the fire-escape landing of the third floor, an old woman stands with a child. The flames are almost reaching the old woman's dress, trapping her and the small girl with her in the corner. The firemen are now working very fast. They try to hose down the flames and move the ladder into position. One fireman runs up the ladder and takes the child to safety. He comes back for the old woman. She refuses to move, at first; it's too scary. But the fire is getting to her, there's no choice. She climbs down, crying and shaking. More fire engines arrive and the superpumper. Our whole block is closed off. The crowd is large—people staring, drinking beer, playing their bongo drums. Some have even stopped repairing their cars and moved in to have a closer look. They have to move back, as hoses bounce spray off the wall and the thick black smoke becomes unbearable. And the cops arrive and push the crowd to the other side of the street. And the entertainment is getting somewhat boring.

A young guy with long hair and a guitar under his arm runs back and forth on the roof of the burning building. He keeps looking down as if he lost something in the crowd. The third floor is now burning as brightly as the second. The tenants are coming out the back way, accompanied by two firemen. They hang on to whatever they consider dearest, mostly their pets. Cats and dogs, and one pretty girl about ten is holding her white rabbit, covering his eyes and stroking him at the same time to calm him down. She herself is crying and her mother is crying. They know everything else is lost . . .

Suddenly, an old man appears above the third-floor inferno and starts climbing out on the fire escape. He must have been sitting in his apartment all this time, praying for the nightmare to pass him by. Useless. Our nightmares don't bypass anybody. He's almost too late. The fire escape is red-hot. Firemen try to hose it down so he can walk across to the ladder. The old man is frightened, he's cursing and waving his hands. He makes it with not one second to spare.

I've seen enough. I tell the kids "Let's go." And we're in the park. A beautiful, wonderful day. The sky so blue and transparent except for the black cloud over Eleventh Street. A great many people in the park. Each in their own section—old Slavic people, hippie types, Puerto Ricans, and so on. As far as I can see, there are no ripoffs. So I can relax too. We stay in the park for a few hours. When we return, our block is still closed off and the building is still burning.

There's going to be another abandoned tenement on Eleventh Street now, the fifth. And sixty or seventy people will be stuck into some welfare hotels and then into some other holes. They'd be out of the East Village for good. And the East Village will be smaller still. That's one way to get out of here.

That same evening, a street gang called Centurion Dragons moved into the abandoned tenement that once housed the Magnolia Coffee Shop. They moved in very quietly, in back of the second floor, half a dozen men and three or four women. From that evening on, the block livened up for a while—many other street-gang members from most of the other gangs on the Lower East Side came to visit at one time or another, and Dragons themselves hung around on the stoop across from my window, drinking, singing, and petting every night until five or six in the morning.

One evening, I watched a spectacle I will not forget. A crowd of about two hundred members of at least a dozen different gangs—Puerto Rican Brothers, Katos Nunchacus, Dynamite Brothers, Screaming Phantoms, Black Spades and the rest—came to witness the punishment of one of their members. I don't know what the guy did; some people said he just wanted to quit his gang. Anyway, he was given five lashes with a wide leather belt ending in a large buckle. The executioner really gave it to him. And everyone counted out loud. At the end, the crowd yelled that he should have five more lashes. And he was given five more. After which, the guy picked up his shirt, wiped the blood off his back, took two steps, and collapsed. Three members of his own gang picked him up and carried him through our empty lot toward Tenth Street. The crowd gradually dispersed.

On Fourteenth Street, several men definitely not from our neighborhood are selling the *Militant*, yelling at the shoppers about Nixon, the war, the revolution, and the oppressed working classes. In the bars—Kiwi II and Frog Pond—the talk centers around soul-searching. One friend of mine is joining a monastery sometime soon. Right now he's involved in the scene that I thought went out with the sixties—he's making it with one woman and on the next mattress three women are making out, and a political meeting is going on in the kitchen. My friend is together now, he takes it all in stride and with some humor. The first time I saw him, he was holding his baby, he had been mugged, his throat was cut, and his blood was dripping on the baby's face. That was a long time ago; even his wife has now remarried.

Another friend is wondering while mixing his methadone with 151 rum, does his girlfriend have VD or doesn't she? And whether he's caught it. In the middle of my tenth beer, another friend runs in, a taxi-driver whose cab has just been ripped off. We run out with him, get into another cab, drive around, look around, nothing. We come back. The guy's coat, money, and radio were in the cab. He also left his keys in the ignition. That's the way it goes. Roberta Flack sings away, and everything is forgotten.

I sit down, play a game of chess, and lose. I can't stay too late—have to get up early, go to the new Contact where I work part-time teaching art to runaways. Tompkins Square Park is empty at three in the morning. My dog runs happily, far ahead of me. We get home without meeting a soul. It's still cold, and last night there was a lot of shooting in and around the park, and that may have something to do with it being empty.

A year or two ago, I drew a pen-and-ink sketch of one of the old women who examine garbage cans in search of food and clothing. There are perhaps two dozen of them left around here and some men. They usually wait around public schools and when the remains of the school lunches are thrown out, they swoop down and pick up the leftovers.

I still have that sketch. For some reason I am reluctant to part with it, even though a few people have wanted to buy it. (Today is Monday after the fire. The winter seems to be over. I am desperately trying to finish this book and it is very heavy because this book cannot have an ending, the life goes on and on and always will, even in death.)

This morning, I saw the old woman again. Her back is bent more than ever before, more madness in her completely yellow eyes. She's still rolling her cart filled with rags and half-eaten peanut-butter sandwiches. And her skinny dog is still faithfully tagging along. I watched her until she got into her building. Then I sat on the stage of the People's Park and talked with a couple of kids I've known for a long time. They are now selling grass (a buck a joint), coke, Quaalude, and methadone. I am amazed at their ingenuity, at the things the kids take off with now that heroin is, thank God, no longer with us. A few mornings ago, as I was teaching runaways, two little girls in my class, both very talented artists, were nodding and couldn't hold their pencils.

"We swallowed a whole bunch of Thorazines," one of them explained.

I couldn't believe it.

"Why did you do a stupid thing like that?" I asked. "First

of all, it does nothing for you, and second, it can really kill you."

"That's all we had," she replied. They were asleep for a couple of days, were only now beginning to come out of it. I got mad, and although I usually don't do it, gave them a lecture they will not soon forget. Later, I realized, her answer was perfectly sensible. Something, anything, is better than nothing. And they didn't care that much about living to worry about death.

I sit in the park a few more minutes, go home, do a few sketches. My typewriter looks at me like a python at a rabbit. I eventually come to it. This typewriter has had quite a history too—it's been ripped off and resold at least six times and it still types. There's so much more I want to say, but I know my limitations. Perhaps another time, when I can see things more clearly. Right now, I just want to do some serious artwork. Maybe I'll get lucky and have a show in a couple of months. I think I am going to throw this typewriter out of the window or make a construction out of it. Stop.

Once There Was a Village